T0247739

Praise for *The Go-to-Market Cheat Code*

"*The Go-to-Market Cheat Code: The Secret to Unlocking B2B Growth* is a right hook to the jaw of status quo marketing! Authors Gray and Wagner provocatively challenge B2B marketing sacred cows that are grazing on our businesses today and provide practical techniques and tools to turn them into profitable relationships. A timely and relevant read for executives and founders looking to unlock more lucrative business partnerships."

—Rich Horwath
New York Times *and* Wall Street Journal *bestselling author of*
Strategic: The Skill to Set Direction, Create Advantage,
and Achieve Executive Excellence

"Justin Gray and Josh Wagner have created a game-changing resource in *The Go-to-Market Cheat Code*. I found this book is full of practical strategies and deep insights into the power of strategic partnerships. Gray and Wagner's expertise shines through every page, making complex concepts accessible and actionable. I highly recommend this book to anyone committed to achieving exceptional results in the B2B landscape."

—R. Craig Coppola
commercial real estate broker and advisor,
founding principal, Lee & Associates Arizona

"After spending 25 years driving growth for some of the world's most respected companies, I understand the challenges of engaging the modern, trust-driven buyer. Fortunately, the code has literally been cracked in this book. *The Go-to-Market Cheat Code* provides insights into building stronger organizations by prioritizing strategic partnerships and driving sustainable revenue growth. I highly recommend this read to all current and aspiring B2B leaders. Justin Gray and his coauthor masterfully show that embracing partners is a true force multiplier for businesses. This strategy requires more than collaboration; it demands a shared Ideal Customer Profile, unwavering trust, and a unified vision of customer impact. Their compelling narrative and practical guidance make this book an indispensable resource for anyone aiming to leverage strategic partnerships for significant growth and success."

—Lauren Goldstein
chief growth officer, Winning by Design

THE GO-TO-MARKET CHEAT CODE

THE SECRET TO UNLOCKING B2B GROWTH

Justin Gray AND Josh Wagner

MANAGING PARTNERS, IN REVENUE CAPITAL

WILEY

Published by John Wiley & Sons, Inc., Hoboken, New Jersey.
Published simultaneously in Canada.

For general information on our other products and services or for technical support, please contact our Customer Care Department within the United States at (800) 762-2974, outside the United States at (317) 572-3993 or fax (317) 572-4002.

Wiley also publishes its books in a variety of electronic formats. Some content that appears in print may not be available in electronic formats. For more information about Wiley products, visit our web site at www.wiley.com.

Library of Congress Cataloging-in-Publication Data

Names: Gray, Justin (Entrepreneur), author. | Wagner, Josh, author.
Title: The go-to-market cheat code : the secret to unlocking B2B growth / by Justin Gray and Josh Wagner.
Description: Hoboken, New Jersey : Wiley, [2025] | Includes index.
Identifiers: LCCN 2024037439 (print) | LCCN 2024037440 (ebook) | ISBN 9781394292103 (cloth) | ISBN 9781394292127 (adobe pdf) | ISBN 9781394292110 (epub)
Subjects: LCSH: Business planning. | Strategic planning. | Success in business.
Classification: LCC HD30.28 .G728 2025 (print) | LCC HD30.28 (ebook) | DDC 658.4/012—dc23/eng/20240910
LC record available at https://lccn.loc.gov/2024037439
LC ebook record available at https://lccn.loc.gov/2024037440

Cover Design: Wiley
Cover Image: © In Revenue Capital, LLC
Author Photos: © In Revenue Capital, LLC
SKY10090941_111324

*To the incredibly uncommon tribe that graced LeadMD
for over a decade, without whom the achievements described
in this book would not have been possible.*

Contents

Foreword   *xi*

Introduction   **1**

1 The Digital Mask   **7**

2 Growth and the Cheat Code   **19**

3 The Top-Down Necessity   **29**

4 How to Set Up Your Own Cheat Code   **41**

5 Customer, Context, and Culture   **55**

6 Partner Ecosystem Nuts and Bolts   **81**

7 Co-Marketing   **91**

8 In the Field   **101**

9 The Relationship Recipe   **117**

10 When It All Goes Wrong   **127**

11 Success and the New Metrics   **137**

12 When It All Goes Right   **149**

13 Insights into Successful Partner Programs   **165**

14 Cash in Time   **173**

Conclusion   187
Appendix: Supplemental Information   191
Notes   195
Acknowledgments   197
About the Authors   199
Index   201

Contents

Foreword

Jon Miller
*MarTech entrepreneur and co-founder at Marketo
and Engagio (acquired by Demandbase)*

As someone who has been in the founder's seat many times – with Marketo, Engagio, and now my latest startup – I've had the opportunity to watch (and perhaps influence) the changing Business-to-Business (B2B) Go-to-Market (GTM) playbook, and I've come to intimately understand the critical importance of trust as the foundation of our GTM strategies.

Building a successful B2B business has never been easy, but the challenges today are greater than ever. Chief marketing officers are struggling to grow pipeline with static budgets. Sales development representatives (SDRs) productivity is plummeting. Overall revenue growth has slowed dramatically. Although the uncertain economic environment is certainly a factor, the root cause is that the old B2B marketing and sales playbooks – which I helped create and promote during my time at Marketo – simply don't work as well as they used to.

These "tried-and-true" playbooks of inbound and outbound marketing emerged with the move to digital in the early 2000s. We created compelling content like definitive guides, whitepapers, and webinars to excite and engage buyers. At the time, they were eager to exchange their contact info for these valuable educational resources. We then nurtured these leads with sophisticated automated email sequences, scored them to attempt to identify who actually was ready to speak with sales, and passed the best ones to eager SDRs for follow-up. Everything was meant to be highly predictable and measurable. The promise of marketing earning a seat at the revenue table had arrived.

But times have changed. Today, the market is overwhelmed by mediocre content. Every company is pumping out blog posts, infographics, and formulaic "thought leadership" pieces that all start to sound the same. (Generative AI is rapidly making this worse.) Buyers are wise to our clever lead-generation tricks. B2B marketers have created too much mediocre content, which has driven buyers away from slick company-produced content of any sort. They're on to us. We've lost their trust and therefore they're no longer coming to us. Response rates are down and customer acquisition costs are up across the board.

It's all too tempting for stressed out marketing and SDR leaders to simply turn up the volume. To bombard prospects with even more generic content, more cold calls, more emails. But this "spray and pray" approach is not the answer. In fact, it destroys trust and relevance, aggravating the core problem.

Now, don't get me wrong. Technology, when used well, can be amazing. Marketing automation, account-based marketing sales engagement – in the right hands, these tools and others are immensely powerful. The problem is that all too often, people take shortcuts. They look for the "easy" path to revenue and wind up misusing or underusing the sophisticated technology they've purchased.

We can't keep doing more of the same and expecting different results. That's the definition of insanity. New times call for new strategies.

As B2B founders, we need to take a step back. We must understand how shifts in buying behavior affect our entire GTM. We have to look beyond market-qualified leads and marketing attribution to consider what truly powers sustainable growth: trust in our brand.

By brand, I'm not talking about colors, fonts, and slogans. Brand is what your target market (and the people they trust) thinks and feels about you when you're not in the room. And in B2B, the most critical brand sentiment is trust; that's why "nobody ever got fired for buying IBM" was one of the strongest B2B brands ever.

Trust, cultivated through authentic relationships, lies at the heart of the new B2B playbook. And it's the central argument of *The Go-to-Market Cheat Code* – in an oversaturated market, insight from trusted peers is the ultimate decision-making shortcut. Timely tactics will come and go, but investing in real human connection, often via strategic partnerships, will never go out of style.

I've known the authors – Justin Gray and Josh Wagner – for years, and they are not armchair philosophers or trend-chasing "thrivers." They're battle-tested B2B operators offering an honest, research-backed dissection of why trust and relationships have always been – and will always be – the true foundations of successful businesses. *The Go-to-Market Cheat Code* will challenge your assumptions, reframe your thinking, and arm you with the hard-won wisdom to build trust systematically, at scale, through partnerships.

The insights and advice in these pages are more valuable than any growth hack. I have no doubt it will help many avoid painful missteps and achieve sustainable success. Enjoy the read – and here's to building unshakable trust with your customers, partners, and the market.

Introduction
Why Us? Thoughts on Why We're Here

Justin Gray
Josh Wagner

We don't belong here. We are not MBAs, we don't hold advanced degrees from prestigious schools, weren't raised in Silicon Valley, and we don't have rich parents. The fact is both of us were raised in the town of Fountain Hills, outside Phoenix, Arizona. Our parents were general contractors; we spent our summers sweeping jobsites and hauling lumber in 120° weather. The only option was work. Hard work.

Our parents exposed us to manual labor early as a critical point of context. We knew where the traditional paths led for us, and therefore we also knew that doing something uncommon was the only way out and into a life that didn't involve framing homes in 100° weather and starting from scratch each time a project completed. Business provided that path less traveled, and although our individual paths diverged right around high school and looked very different, we were both ultimately led to the same place.

Josh's Story

While Justin stayed in Fountain Hills for high school, my parents sent me to a prep school in Phoenix. It was a fantastic experience, and

I built some incredible relationships and ultimately what I believe is one of the best networks in Arizona. I followed that up with fairly mediocre run at Arizona State University (ASU) with a broadcasting degree. Not exactly what you think of in an entrepreneur. However, it was during that time I was urged by a professor to explore the business side of broadcasting, which led to a sales internship at a local radio station and the start of my sales career.

When I graduated from ASU, I didn't want to get a job. I had already grown up in a small business family and that entrepreneurial DNA instilled a hunger to go out on my own. The only problem was I didn't have anything to sell. So, I called my friend who'd dropped out of high school to work for a media production company and told him we were going to start a business. So, with no money, no experience, and no connections we started a media production company!

It was a wild experience. I had to learn the fundamentals on my own. Profit-and-loss statements, balance sheets, cashflow, taxes, 1099, W2 . . . all the things. It was trial by fire, but we did it. It was really hard until we found a niche. We networked our way into a strategic partnership that would be the foundation of our business until we closed the doors. It was that experience that taught me the power of relationships and partnerships in business. That business lasted about five years until my friend and I had an honest conversation with each other, which was that we hadn't actually built a business. We created jobs for ourselves, which was fine, but we both wanted and needed more. Mostly more experience. So, we parted ways.

I went on to work for an established media production company that was pivoting to an e-learning company after they lost 90% of their business from 9/11. My job was to figure out how to convert existing clients to e-learning clients and find new business. What I found was a love for niche vertical markets and partnerships. I found that our e-learning solution was not going to compete in higher education or ever in the corporate e-learning market, so I focused on unsophisticated industries with high compliance. Once I identified some good markets, I realized selling custom e-learning was really hard, so I found industry trainers who had been selling classroom training for years. They had the content I needed to build a niche solution. So I called several, asking them to partner with me. They would provide the content for the courses, we'd provide the distribution, and we'd revenue share with them. I wound up successfully doing this is four separate industries.

During my time with the e-learning company, I reconnected with Justin via LinkedIn, which ultimately led to a lunch together. He was running multiple businesses by this time. One was a payment processing business, the other a marketing automation consultancy. That lunch turned out to be a pivotal point in our relationship. I wound up selling him custom e-learning courses and a learning management system for the payments company, and he introduced me to marketing automation. I wound up hiring his consultancy to help me implement a popular marketing automation tool called Marketo to enable the Go-to-Market (GTM) process for our e-learning company to niche vertical markets.

Fast-forward about three years. I got a text from Justin that said, "I need someone who understands this stuff to help me scale sales." The timing could not have been more perfect. I'd hit my ceiling with the e-learning company. It was time for something new, and this was a great opportunity to build something with someone I know and trust – so I took the leap!

When I started at LeadMD in 2014 I knew very little about the Software-as-a-Service world, and quickly realized I was stepping into

3

Introduction

a new arena. When I began, we had one partner, Marketo. It was my job to build relationships with their sellers so that they would bring me, and our services, into their software deals. I was at LeadMD for nine years with Justin before it was acquired in 2021. During that time I sold over $100 million in professional services and at least triple that in software co-sell. Most important, I built the most meaningful relationships in my career with partners, customers, and colleagues. Those relationships, those Cheat Codes, are the way a small-town kid from Fountain Hills, Arizona, becomes the most nontraditional venture capitalist on the planet!

Justin's Story

Meanwhile, while Josh was at that fancy prep school and Arizona State, I was doing anything I could to get out of Fountain Hills, Arizona. I am fond of saying that "I'm a nobody from nowhere" and that's a very true statement. Although my parents owned their own business, growing up, our family's financial state can best be characterized as "feast or famine" – which ultimately summarized out to what would be considered lower-middle class by income standards. Therefore, when it came time for college, my options were squarely in-state. Tucson was as far from Fountain Hills as the options could get, so I immediately packed up my 1989 Camaro and headed south.

After four years and a major pivot from journalism to business, I narrowly missed graduating with a degree by four language credits – thanks a lot, German. The tuition money waxed dry at this point, so my plan was to graduate with deficiency (which I did) and complete those four German credits at night school while in the workforce (which never happened). Instead, I leveraged my business major with a marketing focus to secure what were some of the worst jobs of my life. I worked for traditional companies in office automation and software for the next six years and spent the majority of that time fighting for a marketing budget and executive buy-in.

What I did gain during that time was an incredibly deep well of skills. Because the companies I worked for viewed marketing as an afterthought, I took it on myself to learn nearly every discipline in marketing – from traditional to digital. If they wouldn't pony up the capital to hire for skills, I would just learn them myself and make it happen. From messaging to design to email and web, I did the jobs of exponentially larger teams but for very little pay. So, when an opportunity suddenly presented itself to join a local startup, I jumped at the chance.

The woman I was dating at the time had gotten into a bit of an argument at a local bar during a night out, about marketing, of all things. The gentleman she was arguing with ultimately offered her a job, which she promptly turned down. In 2006 startups didn't have the shine and pristine they do today. Back then "startup" sounded doomed to fail. Before leaving that evening, she mentioned that she just might know someone desperate enough to consider the offer. A few months later I joined their payment technology company as their first director of marketing. It was there I put my generalist skill set to work, ultimately taking the organization from under $1 million in revenues to well over $100 million. During this stint I also took over the sales team and ran their entire GTM motion as vice president of operations of sales and marketing – not to mention a decent equity stake in the organization, which I sold on my departure in 2009. This was the spark that ultimately enabled me to pursue my entrepreneurial desires.

Over the next year I created four different companies, from software to payments to services. Each of those organizations leveraged what

I had come to understand as a critical mix of GTM horsepower – trusted and curated relationships complemented by well-informed digital marketing. This has been the Cheat Code in all of my successes: empowered by great talent, it has ultimately enabled me to start and exit five organizations via highly profitable acquisitions.

Throughout this book you are going to hear from both me and Josh, in almost a ping-pong format. I typically lead with a chapter on strategy, and Josh follows it up with a chapter on translating those strategies to actionable tactics. Along the way we tell a lot of stories, share a lot of examples, and introduce you to some great people we met along the way.

We hope you enjoy *The Go-to-Market Cheat Code*.

Chapter 1

The Digital Mask

Justin Gray

You've been lied to. Not intentionally and not maliciously, but even so. The truth has been distorted, and countless startup founders like you have made critical business decisions based on flawed information. For too long, the Business-to-Business (B2B) play-book has been written to be a programmatic, technology-dependent series of steps, that when executed with precision, will yield predictable results. That's simply not true.

The story has gone like this. As the internet and the rise of everything digital exploded, buyer behavior changed. Buyers have started living, breathing, and eating online. They're immersed in a world composed of bits and bytes, so much so that they've begun to accomplish much of what used to be conducted in face-to-face (or at least verbal) conversations, absent such interaction.

The Technological Paradigm Shift

In B2B transactions, this is a fundamental shift that flips everything you traditionally think of in the realm of "selling" on its head. Completely upending decades of approach, process, and thinking, this paradigm shift is encapsulated in a single statistic that launched thousands of software companies and consultancies alike: the fact that, in 2023, the modern B2B buyer was said to spend 67% of their buying journey with their chosen brands online. Further bolstering the digital push is the prediction that the figure will increase as much as 80%.[1]

What's more, they were doing so largely unknown to you. About 60% were said to be poking around your website, 55% attending your webinar, 52% researching you and similar solutions, and 50% evaluating you on peer review sites before they'd accept an actual "sales meeting."

Marketers everywhere have read these statistics over and over and over again, and it transformed an entire business model. Since the early 2010s, stats like this have permeated the headspace of CEOs, product teams, marketers, and sellers alike – and they've responded in kind, working tirelessly to transform digitally and accommodate what is seen as the new normal.

If you speak to any Go-to-Market (GTM) leader today, it's rare that you can get beyond the first couple minutes of the conversation without hearing how they are prioritizing digital strategies and tactics. These conversations almost always reveal their own personal innovations for how they intend to stand out in what has become a very noisy crowd.

Over the last couple of decades, startups and global enterprises alike have fundamentally shifted their budgets to ensure they had a big enough slice of the digital pie, fearing the repercussions of being branded as digital laggards. Almost every trend and tactic in the last 20 years reflects this.

Note: In 2010, digital marketing accounted for 24% of overall marketing spend, and now, just a little over a decade later, it's not uncommon for companies to spend three quarters of their marketing budgets on digital marketing.[2] The pandemic only amplified this trend further and, in 2023, 82% of organizations reprioritized offline investments toward digital channels.

Companies have, ubiquitously, placed their hope in digital advertising, social media advertising, search engine optimization, content marketing, and beyond. Of course they did. It's what all the research firms, savvy business leaders, surveys, reports, and statistics told them to do.

But what if these trends and bold declarations were ultimately lies? Or, more accurately, what if they were short-sighted and even self-serving? What if they failed to paint the full picture of what's really going on in the business landscape today?

Speculate no further, because this is exactly what has happened. As practitioners who have helped thousands of organizations navigate the waters of B2B digital marketing and sales since the new millennium, we think it's even more important to understand why fickle, yet pervasive shifts like this take place.

Fundamentally, the inbound and outbound demand strategies on which the growth plans of many modern companies are based are built not to serve the successful growth of the adopter, but instead to serve the success of vendors that facilitate those strategies. These are modern maxims literally created on the misleading idea that digital channels are everything.

Because vendor content and sponsored research told them to do so, they created their approach based on the idea that people don't *want* to talk to vendors. Although there's some truth to this, it's again an incomplete snapshot of what's really going on.

Trust Has Always Been Paramount

The more complete picture is that people don't want to talk to sources they don't trust. People have always sought out relationships they trust, and this remains as true today as it ever has been.

So, although buyers still seek out trusted sources for recommendations and information, the digital channels initially positioned as the de facto forum for credible information exchange are suddenly and rapidly decreasing in effectiveness. They're just not generating ready-to-buy leads any longer – and arguably, they never were.

When these tactics were at their most effective, they were new. From roughly 2005 to 2012, digital approaches had novelty working in their favor, coupled with a lack of saturation. But most important, trust was granted by proxy. If someone publishes information online, that information must be trustworthy, right? The statement sounds comical today, and it is indeed dripping with naivete – but we all flocked to these "too-good-to-be-true" channels.

Everything was new and exciting, from digital ads to email marketing, content in every form and beyond. No longer did the size of your office building or expensive presence at industry events reflect the tenure and success of your organization. Instead, your web presence told that tale, a billboard with a much lower cost and fewer barriers to creation. We could all suddenly be positioned as who we wanted to be, with a few strokes of the keyboard.

When I launched one of my companies, a digital marketing consultancy called LeadMD, we ran a general email nurture series that extended for an entire year. Every two weeks, we'd send a piece of content to prospects in our database. You'd be amazed by the number of people who responded to those emails saying we read their thoughts because of how relevant our topics were.

In actuality, we were just putting out our own best practices on how to perform the hottest digital tactics being advertised by software vendors, who coincidentally had created applications necessary to perform the digital tactics they were amplifying. Everyone was reading from the same hymnal, and it was very evident.

So yes, inbound and outbound tactics seemed magical in the beginning. They were akin to arriving early at a party. The only people at the party were the ones you actually wanted to talk to, and you had time to have great conversations and eat and drink all of the good stuff before the unwelcome masses arrived. But just like that party, eventually everyone else shows up, and it's a mess. At some point, all you want to do is go home and watch Netflix.

When Digital Tactics Went Stale

The party got dull about 2015. B2B demand generation continued to evolve, largely driven by the need to accommodate more functionality and more tools, and just like before, this was influenced highly by the content marketing engines of companies who wanted to sell the requisite software. But at this point, digital tactics weren't being used by *some* marketers; they were being heavily adopted by all GTM professionals, marketers, sellers, customer service teams, and product organizations – and buyers had started to become wary, to say the least.

Traditional Tactics Are Alive and Well

The digital touchpoints marketers relied on only told a fragment of the story. In fact, the most important elements of that story were often completely invisible. Although we relied on the same digital best practices we preached day in and day out at my consultancy for our own GTM efforts, we never did so independent from our traditional efforts. They were inseparably threaded. The fundamental relationship motions I had always implemented at my past ventures, and at LeadMD for our best clients, were still there – and what's more, the traditional tactics were often the tactics that really drove results.

When a prospect responded to a digital campaign, they would still communicate that they had spoken to a current client, or one of our partners, or had seen us co-present with one of their vendor relationships. They were engaging with us through a digital channel, but they were informing their decision to do so by actually talking with other humans. There was something else going on that wasn't reflected on the shiny attribution reports marketing would generate.

The pandemic was the big test for what has become known as digital transformation. I think COVID-19 is somewhat of a "JFK" moment for the generations who worked jobs highly affected by the global pandemic. I certainly remember where I was when we made the decision to shut down our offices and send people home.

As a digitally native organization, this in and of itself was not the biggest worry on my mind. Setting aside the culture and operational ramifications, not to mention what became a sidelining of the "in-office" environment, the most significant ramification of the pandemic was its ability to call us on our bullshit.

B2B had spent the better part of two decades claiming the buying and selling process had truly gone digital native – and this was checkmate. Would we be ready? Could we all be effective at the strategies we had been preaching and supposedly practicing with surgical precision? We'll never know. Without fail, and through the entire lockdown aspect of the pandemic and still through today, all every organization tried to do was re-create the energy of face-to-face interactions, predominantly failing at the task.

What we learned was incredibly important, but largely ignored. Since the early heyday of digitally enabled inbound/outbound, the promise of "better" by orders of magnitude hasn't materialized. Those tactics that blazed new trails in the mid-2000s are largely the same today.

Where we had expected a pace of rapid innovation, we got degrees of improvement. And fractions of uptick don't have the same wow factor the digital windfalls did in the beginning. At the center of this slowed innovation resides the buyer. Demand fuels supply and all it takes is a quick conversation with, well anyone, to uncover that people – not just buyers, but people – are digitally overwhelmed. The supply has greatly outpaced demand. We dogpiled on the potential, and we squashed it.

Consumers Are Wiser Now

For their part, buyers (e.g. consumers) are disenfranchised. They've caught on to the fact that the same helpful folks pumping out a never-ending stream of helpful content, best practices, and frameworks are incentivized by the action their content suggests. They don't want to get sucked into sales processes. The whole concept of content marketing has been largely redacted to simply "marketing," exposing the thin covering of leaves disguising the sales deadfall that lurks below – and they all know what's at the bottom of that pit.

So, whether you're trying to push (outbound) or pull (inbound) interest into your product, buyers know that both options equate to interruption. Advertising interrupts someone from what they're actively doing or planning to do. Digital campaigns and events interrupt their work, their attention, and their lives. Because of this, many buyers have reverted to operating like they did before the self-proclaimed "rise of digital." They're turning to trusted individuals who have done it before, with whom they have relationships. Buyers simply can't trust what's online.

The Startup Landscape

The startup landscape has changed just as much. Previously, you had to be super scrappy to get a Series A funding, but now, you can blow the whole war chest on cost per lead. The thinking was that spending a dollar would get you a lead. If you threw more money and bodies and technology at a company, there would be a corresponding yield – which would amplify and take you to unicorn status. Obviously, this was based on a false foundation.

As a result, Venture capital (VC) firms have widely started investing in companies more like private equity firms do: at a multiple of revenues, or in some cases the true bottom line, in the form of Earnings Before Interest, Taxes, Depreciation, and Amortization (EBITDA), rather than a "what-if?" valuation. If there's no path to profitability, you haven't embraced the latest trend, which sounds a lot more like something your grandfather might tout: "efficient growth."

What's the first budget line item to be cut? You guessed it. The same line item that was positioned as "the answer" just years prior: marketing. And it's not getting better. All your efforts are getting less and less effective, which is eroding more and more of your bottom line.

It's hard out there. There just seems to be no way out, no way to get to the next stage. A lot of VC money is drying up because they're not confident that these organizations can ultimately reach the public markets. In other words, the outcome everyone has been aiming toward isn't reliable anymore.

No Customer Buys Without Trust

So, with all this in mind, what's left? If digital isn't the magic bullet it was presented to be, what is? You need a window into organizations to understand what they're struggling with and where their acute pain is – and you need someone to bring you into the circle of trust within that organization.

This is where a bit of Josh's and my own personal histories are relevant. Despite our joint desire to ensure this book doesn't devolve into a long and highly detailed résumé, this inclusion is certainly more than relevant.

I've spent the lion's share of my professional life as an entrepreneur. This includes building my own organizations, which I've done five times now, ultimately garnering successful exits by way of acquisition for all five. It also includes the fact that one of my ventures was a services business that assisted in building thousands of businesses by proxy.

In contemplating my next go-around, I looked back at where success and failure diverged. Leveraging those firsthand insights took me back to my strongest realizations, which had come at the height of the digital marketing revolution. I couldn't shake what had become a splinter in my mind for many years. No matter how adept we became at digital demand generation, no one bought without checking a critical box. That box was *trust*.

In mid-June 2023, Josh and I met for breakfast. What was truly on the menu that day was the desire to create a new type of VC firm, which is actually the least relevant point when it comes to this book and topic. I had formulated a concept that we now call *Operator-Immersive Capital*, which for all intents and purposes just means we pay to work really hard. Anytime we make a seed stage investment, our team also steps in to grow and scale the GTM motion.

How we intended to do this is, as they say, where the rub comes in. Josh had been operating on the front lines of our own GTM motion at LeadMD and had seen the same critical relationship between success and trust that I had. This ultimately became the core of our thesis for the capital firm we founded; we would invest only within startups that had the presence or potential to unlock strategic relationships as a fundamental GTM channel. Then, we would help them grow and scale that channel as their primary path to success.

This might include partners, but it can also be advisors or personal relationships. Regardless of type, the goal is to tap into the trust that's already established there. In most cases, this circle will be small. In fact, in the same way that individuals can only manage about five core friendships, most organizations will have one, maybe two, truly strategic partners.

"A million points of data that show that things that used to work don't work as well anymore. However, teams keep pumping all this money into these spam cannon software solutions and it doesn't make sense. I think that the Go-to-Market approach is dying and it has to be replaced by a Go-to-Network approach. I think in the future, the only way you're gonna be able to open opportunities is because of who you know."– Scott Leese, CEO and founder, Scott Leese Consulting

To drive efficient and sustainable revenue growth in your business, you need to activate what often lurks in the background, just beyond the line of sight in those glossy marketing dashboards – real, trusted relationships. If trust is the new gold, then relationships are the new prospector. That's what we had seen consistently in helping to unlock revenues at some of the largest and most recognizable brands on the planet and inside of our own businesses. That was the x factor.

Tip: To drive efficient and sustainable revenue growth, you need to understand the buyer explicitly, then find the concentric circles of trust that exist between you and a potential partner. This is the basis for creating a successful relationship ecosystem.

Don't allow yourself to fall prey to the digital lies that have been built by incomplete statistics and self-serving vendors trying to sell you on the latest fad. The fact is, digital effectiveness continues to decline. Relationships have been here forever: person-to-person recommendations, conversations, insights, and partnerships. They're the tools we lean on when we make substantive purchases in our own personal lives – and we don't lose our humanity when we buy on behalf of our businesses.

Despite the false narratives perpetuated across most of this millennium, buyers are humans. Humans don't buy exclusively online, they don't even buy exclusively from people they like, but they do buy from people they trust, every time. This very human desire for authentic relationships and trusted information are the only tools that truly unlock demand and growth.

Relationships are the currency of success, and establishing trust makes all the difference between capturing alpha or falling behind.

Chapter 2

Growth and the Cheat Code

Josh Wagner

Up, up, down, down, left, right, left, right, B, A, start. If you grew up in the 1980s, you remember this sequence as the 30 lives Cheat Code for the game *Contra* on the original Nintendo Entertainment System. For those who didn't . . . Google it!

If digital is no longer the cheat it was in the early 2000s and relationships are the new prospector, what's the new Cheat Code? It might be counterintuitive to think of relationship building as a cheat, but that is the premise of this chapter.

The Partnership Ecosystem

McKinsey[1] predicts that within the next two or three years, partnership ecosystems will represent 30% of the global economy. That's up from 1–2% today. There were also some impressive stats that came out of the first Partnership Leader Catalyst conference in Miami in 2022. According to partner-led growth champion and industry pioneer Allan Adler,[2] who you will hear more from in this book,

> The conference was amazing, as are some of the data that is coming out on Partner Ecosystem performance. Their

data suggests that account mapping and other tools help B2B SaaS [Software-as-a-Service] partnership teams crush it with their tech partnerships by:

- Boosting their win rate by 41%

- Increasing their average deal size by 43%

- Generating two times the revenue

Even so, partnerships can mean a lot of things in Business-to-Business (B2B) SaaS. Ask 10 "partner people" how they define partnerships and you'll get 10 different answers. Some might consider channel partnerships the primary kind of partner, and others might think of partnerships in terms of relationships with suppliers or technology providers.

We host a podcast called *The Cheat Code*, on which we interview the best and brightest Go-to-Market (GTM) leaders. What we've learned is that, when it comes to partnerships, the definition is consistently inconsistent.

We define a *partner* broadly as another organization whose people hold trusted relationships with the customers we want to acquire. It's as simple as that, and the key word is *relationship*.

According to Jay McBain and Forrester, 76% of world trade is indirect,[3] meaning it happens through partnerships. The food you eat, the car you drive, and the clothes you wear all happen through manufacturing, distribution, and sales channel partnerships.

But in the B2B SaaS world, that isn't the norm, except for a few companies like Salesforce, HubSpot, and Shopify, which have grown through the partner ecosystems they have built around them. That's changing.

SaaS companies are recognizing that the strategies of the past digitized sales and marketing automations aren't delivering the cheap customer acquisition of the past. Can the Cheat Code be the pivot?

Consider this hypothetical situation. Imagine that the Microsoft of today was selling its products directly, not through the partner eco-system of more than 400 000 partners who employ 22 million people and deliver more than $10 in economic value for every dollar of Microsoft revenue, worldwide.[4]

What if that partner ecosystem didn't exist? Envision instead that Microsoft had a massive team of salespeople, and an equally massive marketing effort designed to drive direct leads to those salespeople who called on customers. The impact is not the same. The reason the partner ecosystem at Microsoft is so successful is that Microsoft leverages the most powerful thing their partner has: the relationship with the customer.

That relationship provides the partner proximity to the customers' problems and the trust required to provide a solution. Microsoft pro-vides a host of products, all of which can be molded by the partner to meet the needs of the customer. Creating that level of trust at scale is untenable without a robust partner network.

According to Jared Fuller, one of the leading voices in the partner ecosystem movement and founder of PartnerHacker, "Bessemer Venture Partners was quoted as saying in 2021, 'Do not invest in a partner program until you're past $100 million in revenue.' Then, the very next year – 2022 – their number one recommendation in the Bessemer State of the Cloud annual report was partner-led growth, calling it table stakes from day one."[5] How quickly things change.

Changing the Narrative

Folks like us at In Revenue Capital, Jared, and many others you'll meet throughout this book are leading the movement behind the Partnership Cheat Code and are catalysts for changing the narrative of the traditional partner program.

Digital has failed to deliver, inbound and outbound are failing, yet expectations from investors continue to rise. Account Executive quota attainment is at an all-time low. Sellers who once lived on inbound during the golden age of content marketing have gone the way of the dodo bird due the oversaturation of mediocre and flat-out bad content put into the market by B2B marketing teams.

The response to the lack of inbound has been a flood of outbound. Armies of sales development representatives are being hired to pound phones like a scene from the film *Boiler Room*. It doesn't stop there. The rise of sales technology, which looks remarkably like marketing technology, has given this eager bunch license to blast automated email sequences to the masses. And marketing is not the only department responsible for spam.

Giving to Get Mindset

The Partnership Cheat Code is one that adds value to *all* who are involved. It's a give-to-get mentality focused on leveraging existing relationships to accelerate growth. This thinking can be applied to our Venture capital (VC) firm as well as the early-stage companies like those in our portfolio.

"When I got an opportunity to run partnerships in one of my earlier roles, it was my lightbulb moment. I liked sales, but sales always felt very transactional to me. I enjoyed creating genuine connections and relationships rather than transactional sales. Partnerships were the best of both worlds. I saw that it was sales but also building long-term, genuine strategic relationships with people. And because it resonated with who I am, I excelled at it."

– Greg Portnoy, cofounder and CEO, EULER

Here are the three main ingredients a startup needs to be successful:

- **Capital:** This is money, usually from investors, that you get to keep the ball rolling when money from operations isn't yet enough to fuel growth.

- **Strategy:** This is where you decide what that ball is, how to roll it, where to roll it, and when.

- **Execution:** Put simply, this is the part where you work your tail off to keep that ball rolling faster and faster to drive revenue.

Then apply our Cheat Code and you will quickly see a divergence from the traditional VC model, which is focused on deploying capital. The founders are left to find their way with strategy and execution. The way traditional VC firms look at their portfolio is centered on fund dynamics, a concept we take a deep dive into in Chapter 14 of this book. For now, let's focus on strategy and execution.

When a founder closes a round of funding, it's a big deal. It could mean critical hires, it could mean product upgrades and, frankly, it could mean they live to fight another day. The one thing it means without question is that the company is expected to GROW! Seed stage companies that take on VC financing are typically expected to grow between 100% and 300% year over year.

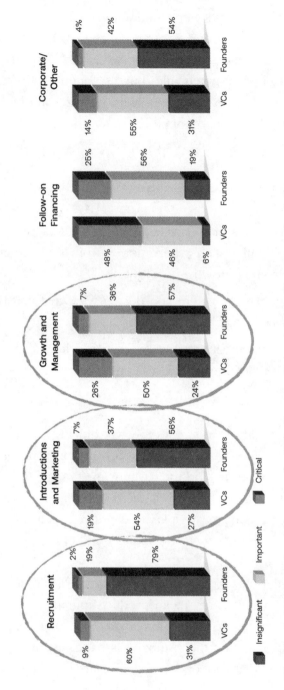

Figure 2.1 Perceived impact of a VC. *Source:* Copyright In Revenue Capital.

That's no small feat, especially given the state of traditional GTM functions like inbound and outbound. Founders typically expect their new capital partners will support them in that growth, be it referrals, recruiting, or potentially operational support, only to find that they are ill-equipped to do so (see Figure 2.1).

Here's why. At Stanford, UC Berkeley, or any number of Ivy League universities, where venture capitalists tend to get their finance degrees, company operations are not a focus. So, for the most part, these investors "know" operations theoretically, maybe from textbooks or, for the more seasoned, by watching from the sidelines.

They might have some answers, but they don't have the actual experience to back up those answers or provide any real business wisdom that comes from doing the work. At the end of the day, the job of a venture capitalist is to finance businesses to generate a return, not to operate them.

The other factor at play is what we call *the blockbuster movie model*. The one mega-million-dollar box office smash pays for all the other box office losers. Unfortunately, this is very similar to the way a traditional VC fund operates. In fact, these funds evaluate companies based on their ability to "return the fund."

This is a dynamic that does not incentivize investors to help founders operate; rather, it encourages a focus on placing more bets to increase their odds. If the key to growth is more than capital, where do we turn? This is the core tenet of the *operator immersive model*, which Justin and I created based on our experience building businesses leveraging our Cheat Code.

Driving Efficient Growth

There is no shortage of VC, private equity, growth equity, or other capital firms out there, but if you filter by those run by experienced operators, the list gets significantly shorter. Filter even further by those who work in the business side by side, day in and day out with the founder – shorter yet. Finally, add the filter of experienced GTM operators who have grown and scaled via partnership . . . that's a very short list. Bootstrapped, funded or otherwise, every founder is looking for efficient ways to drive growth.

I used the Microsoft example previously because it's a household name, but as a startup founder you might be thinking the Microsoft example just isn't relatable to you. I get that, but it sets the stage for a much more relatable example – one that Justin and I lived firsthand as we built LeadMD on the back of a single strategic partner in the early days and scaled to a full ecosystem leading to our exit in 2022.

From day one, Justin modeled LeadMD, a professional services business, as if it were a modern SaaS business. Thirty percent year-over-year growth was our North Star metric, a high-water mark in the services world. We had a sales team, a rarity in professional services and consulting. We had a marketing team, also a rarity in this world.

Direct sales outbound in services is really, really hard. Trust me, I've done it. Inbound has legs for sure and we had tremendous marketing leadership that built a substantial inbound engine, but the linchpin for our sales and marketing efforts was our core partner, Marketo.

Our team (our product) comprised the foremost experts in Marketo and everything that surrounded Marketo. We loved to tout that we knew Marketo better than Marketo knew Marketo. That strategic partnership was the anchor of our GTM strategy. We were in the service of the customer.

We liked to say that we spoke the language of the chief marketing officer, meaning we knew their mind and had the proximity, relationships, and trust with the target Marketo customer base, which enabled us to be the best possible partner. The executive-level messaging combined with deep expertise on the platform helped propel us as a Top Marketo Partner each year, leading to our 30% year-over-year growth target.

Businesses grow or die, especially in startup land. Growth today is harder than ever; the lies of digital continue to persist, inbound and outbound alone are not meeting targets. The customer is faced with more and more noise. If trust is the new gold, where should we mine?

Partnerships

Partnerships are the Cheat Code Microsoft uses to remain as one of the top companies in the world, the Cheat Code we used at LeadMD both for our own success as well as that of our clients, and the Cheat Code of the GTM leaders you will be introduced to in this book. Finally, they are the Cheat Code best-in-class businesses are leveraging to win, in an era that recognizes the fact that the old "predictive growth" playbook simply no longer works.

Chapter 3

The Top-Down Necessity

Justin Gray

The most common question we get from startups and mature organizations alike is how to get started. Given the surge in popularity for partnerships and ecosystem-led growth, even enterprise companies that have long histories surrounding their "partnership programs" are looking for a reboot.

The thread that connects startups and mature organizations alike is learning from the mistakes of those who came before them, to ensure they aren't doomed to repeat them.

CEOs have historically held ecosystems (and the teams responsible for creating and maintaining them) at an arm's length in a desire for what I would categorize as plausible deniability. There have been highly visible examples of modern Software-as-a-Service organizations, like Microsoft and Salesforce.com, building strong technology partnerships that have seemingly fed the Go-to-Market (GTM) success of these organizations, simply due to their presence.

But it's equally important that we don't overlook who those companies were – category creators like Microsoft and Salesforce.com – and who represented entire shifts in the way Business-to-Business worked and sold. Therefore, integration and the commercialization of those providers went hand-in-hand. This dynamic was overlooked and therefore executive teams laid down the edict that their companies do the same, but with little alignment and top-down support for the spirit and latticework necessary to drive success in more competitive environments.

Today, CEO and organization-wide support is critical in developing a thriving ecosystem-led culture. In fact, it's so ubiquitous that nearly every single guest on Josh's and my podcast, *The Cheat Code*, has cited it as a mission-critical ingredient in building and executing a successful partner ecosystem.

> "You need to be open-minded and collaborative. You can't just rely on getting paid for referrals because it doesn't work like that. You have to find other ways to motivate and reward people. This different mindset is challenging for some channel professionals. You can't force these tech partners to act since they aren't paid per transaction. So, how do you incentivize them?"
>
> – Chris Samila, cofounder and Chief Partner Officer,
> Partnership Leaders

So, in this chapter, we tackle this precursor to partnerships head-on. We also dig into the underlying mentality that is so fundamental to unlocking ecosystem-led growth that proceeding without it condemns these programs to failure.

Starting at the Top

For the partner ecosystem to work, you can't simply put anyone in charge of partnerships. There must be buy-in – and direction – from the top, or there won't be buy-in anywhere else. The ideal scenario is having someone seasoned in the CEO role who really grasps the value of partnerships and can put the horsepower of the organization in line with that belief.

Of course, it's not enough for the CEO to tell their team that partners matter; each different area of the business needs to understand what that translates into for them. In each area, your team must understand that their contributions to the partner ecosystem are mission-critical. They should know, concretely, what it is they need to do to drive this forward and what their Key performance indicator (KPI) or measure of success is.

To reach that goal, each department should work through these questions:

- What is our group's partnership goal?
- What are the motions we will take to ensure we achieve partner integration at a fundamental level?

Let's take a look at how this might shake out in the most common departments.

Sales

Sales is the frontline of each organization and is responsible for the acquisition of new customer relationships. For these groups, establishing trust is paramount but equally difficult to do because buyers are well aware of their primary motivator: money. Are the suggestions of a sales executive truly in the best interest of the buyer? Will their proposed solutions actually solve the problems the buyer cares about? These are difficult walls to break down, given that buyers are strongly influenced by their past experiences, many of which are bound to be poor. As such, partnerships can provide access to that critical trust element via the transference of the partner's preexisting relationship – much in the same way a friend might vouch for another when first meeting members of an established group.

Marketing

Marketing is always a hotly contested function, but I think that for these purposes we can agree that the role of marketing is to foster awareness and trust within the target customer, both pre- and post-sale. With this charge, marketing benefits from partner ecosystems in many of the same ways sales does, but at an even greater scale. Brands take years to successfully establish, and thus the power of a brand can be an immense benefit when latched on to by an earlier stage organization or an organization that is not known for doing or being a certain thing.

Partnerships create proxy perceptions that are highly transferable among the involved partners. Beyond market perception, marketing partnerships can also provide much needed horsepower to fill gaps within each of the participating partners. We saw this play out time and time again at LeadMD, where we had an incredible amount of skill at our disposal. Often we would incentivize co-marketing campaigns through the provision of all the necessary legwork. Our operational prowess enabled us to move quickly, with a high degree of quality. This was extraordinarily beneficial to even the largest of brands. Large partners were more than willing to lend their cache in exchange for operational execution they could not provide due to competing priorities.

Customer Success

By now we've seen the symbiotic value of partners, and customer success is the capstone of this mentality because it informs both sales and marketing via the creation of value, which can fuel all GTM efforts. From integration partners that expand or fill gaps a software platform might have in delivering against a customer use case, to services partners that ensure adoption and achievement of a solution, customer success is the root of any solid customer value proposition. By leveraging partners, organizations are able to establish two absolute keys to success:

- First is focus. By embracing what you are and what you are not enables you to focus your time and resources while becoming a true master of your chosen craft.

- Second, by curating partnerships for your customer's use case, you become far more than simply a cog in the machine. Instead you are the connection point among a proven cohort of trusted players all laser focused on driving a successful (and measurable) outcome. The trust bestowed in the marketing and sales processes must be paid off during customer success. This is a cyclic process that drives the customer relationship deeper and provides license to bestow the trust you've earned on other partners, thus driving the ecosystem.

Siloed Partnerships Are Failed Partnerships

When the partnerships in your organization are run in a siloed way, they always fail. This usually happens when the CEO or other top leaders don't recognize the value of partnerships, and they think of them as a program that's disconnected from everything else. They see it as a partner program, not a company-wide mentality of embracing partnerships in service and augmentation of everyone's core responsibilities.

The only person who can reverse this type of setup is the CEO. But they can't do it single-handedly because their role encompasses so much else. Instead, they'll need to assemble a really strong partnership team or leaders within the different areas of their business who "get it." These individuals are essentially the partnership ambassadors, and they can take the message and translate it to their team members and solve issues when they arise.

Leadership and Visibility

The CEO should expect to be driving the partner initiative like they would drive any core initiative of business. So, if your churn is an issue or you're rolling out a new product, your visibility as the CEO backing the partnership initiative is incredibly critical. At the same time, it's also crucial that you're introducing the partnership leader and the partnership team as drivers of the business. Let other employees know how to reach out to them and what they can go to them for.

Furthermore, they should facilitate success down the chain of command. For instance, if someone's team is underperforming, they might need to hop in and resolve that issue. But there also needs to be a deputy relationship with the partner leader so that people understand that they matter and that they are acting on the CEO's directives.

Tip: Ultimately, your partner leader should be thought of as a fundamental executive on your team, whether they're in the C-suite or not. This is how important their role is and how much the CEO needs to back them publicly and vocally.

The CEO can create an insights-driven decision-making culture by ensuring partners are recorded in all core data systems. When this happens, everyone on the team should be able to look in your systems of record, like your customer relationship management (CRM) system, for example, and see what deals you're working on with partners. They should have visibility that enables them to see which partners are engaged with each one of their customers. This increases transparency and enables everyone to be involved – and invested – in the partnership ecosystem.

Finding a Strategic Alliance

On our *Cheat Code* podcast, we talked with Jared Fuller, the Chief Revenue and Partner Officer at Reveal, producer and cohost of the *Nearbound* podcast, and author of *The Partner Hacker Handbook* and *Nearbound: The Book*. He gave us some excellent insights into what it takes to identify and create strategic alliance opportunities, and how a CEO can coach their team to find the right kinds of partners.

Jared says that, when looking for strategic alliance opportunities, you have to first determine what's most valuable to the potential partner and how you can affect that better than the other partners in some way. To that end, here's his recommended formula for finding a strategic alliance. If you're a CEO, it's up to you to teach your team to find partners who care about finding the answers to these questions, too.

- What is most important to the company (e.g. a top-three metric for the CEO)?
- How do you affect that metric?

- What does your impact on that metric look like at scale?
- Who in the company is compensated based on that metric?

Jared talked about an example that allowed him to win a much coveted partnership with HubSpot. He had identified that the most important metric within Hubspot's sales division was ensuring free-to-paid conversions on the HubSpot CRM platform – because HubSpot CRM had launched with a "free" pricing tier and getting those customers to monetize was a strategic initiative. Well, Jared also discovered that the best indicator of a customer's propensity to convert from a free to a paid plan was their ability to actually win a deal in the CRM they were effectively piloting for free. This made sense; buyers are more apt to pay for tools they are using success- fully where they can attribute value to its use. He then created a way for PandaDoc users to seamlessly integrate HubSpot data into e-sign forms, which in turn helped those unpaid users close more deals and pave the road for them to become paid users. From there, he presented the data he collected from this experiment to HubSpot's Vice President of Product. It was a huge win for HubSpot and it was a huge win for Jared's company at the time, PandaDoc. Great partnerships are always value-forward, meaning you provide value as a means of securing and maintaining the partnership – and if that value is a top priority for the leadership team, all the more effective.

Creating a successful partnership requires an entrepreneurial-minded approach because there are best practices but no rulebook. The cre- ative solutions needed to build a thriving partnership come from considering the entire business of each party and how to have an impact on what matters most.

To be successful in a partnership role, you need to remain curious about the market, customer, and industry to uncover a truly powerful joint value proposition. You also need courage to go to your leadership team and explain why you want to go all-in on a partnership. And, finally, you need the conviction to be willing to die on that hill, which takes guts and a well-informed decision.

Partner Compensation

This is another aspect of partnership ecosystems that needs to be driven from the top down. To start, partner compensation must be tied directly to the organization's revenue health. Traditional KPIs serve as the foundation for evaluating partnership effectiveness, but it's important to look beyond simply tracking revenue directly generated by partners. Instead, focus on sourced and influenced revenue, which reflects the true impact of partnerships.

Core business metrics – bookings goals, sales velocity, Annual Contract Value, churn rates, and net churn – they establish the baseline for partnership evaluation. From there, you can identify how partnerships elevate these metrics. Tracking partner attachment rates are a great foundation, and improvements on baseline metrics can then form the basis for variable compensation. You want to ensure you have a complete picture of where and when your partners are engaged across your GTM life cycle.

Variable compensation tied to performance improvement incentivizes partnership success, especially in established businesses. For organizations below $50 million in revenue, it's essential for driving growth. It ensures that partnership goals align with individual incentives, fostering a culture of accountability and performance.

Effective partnership management requires alignment from top to bottom. Understanding the leading indicators necessary for partnership maturity enables us to set appropriate goals. Integrating an adjustable lever within sales compensation plans, such as an increase in compensation rate paid when partners are involved in a successful sale, provides flexibility for driving partnership adoption and proactivity.

For example, setting a target of 100% partner attachment in all new deals could trigger additional compensation incentives. By aligning sales and customer success incentives with partnership objectives, we motivate teams to prioritize and excel in partnership activities, driving mutual success and organizational growth.

You really need the foresight of someone in that CEO position to look ahead and recommend augmenting the comp plan so that you can foster these behaviors within the organization. Then, you can transition to a more traditional partner sourced or influenced revenue down the road, once people have adopted the motion involving not only a partner but also the right partner within their processes.

By then, you should have some metrics to show that your deals are moving faster or getting larger. This is the way you really change the behaviors of the organization: show them success in the form of results. Without these proof points, teams want to bring in a partner only when a customer is explicitly asking for something that requires a third party, often a system integration or perhaps implementation. When lacking the concrete proof, they have the perception that a partner will slow them down or add complexities.

The truth, though, is that complexity will naturally arise down the road if a problem is uncovered that a partner could solve, yet it's left unresolved for the sake of winning the sale quickly. For example, you find that a prospect's marketing database is disorganized and incomplete; yet, rather than leveraging your partner ecosystem to engage a consultant or service partner to help, instead you gloss over the issue and proceed with the sale of marketing software. You'll see that problem resurrected eventually and often in greater magnitude, either in the churn of that customer or the success of the implementation or their lack of results tied to the use of your technology. So, rather than kicking the can down the road with disastrous outcomes, all you're doing is exposing that would-be issue earlier on and in turn becoming a trusted advisor to your prospect – not to mention the goodwill you've created within partner ecosystem.

If you're really able to do this consultative sales motion and figure out all the different pains that could potentially affect the success of your offering, you can then proactively bring in partners to head those off. This will provide a windfall of value, not always right up front, but you'll start to see those trends emerge when you realize that deals are getting large or moving faster, or your win rate is higher.

It's worth repeating that all of this, inclusive of bringing a partner ecosystem model to life, requires deep buy-in from the executive team and a partner mindset from the top down – start there.

Chapter 4

How to Set Up Your Own Cheat Code

Josh Wagner

In the words of the mighty Led Zeppelin, "The Song Remains the Same." If you forgot what you read in Chapter 3, it's worth revisiting. Where do you start? Executive buy-in. Where do you go from there? Glad you asked.

> "As an aspiring entrepreneur wanting to tap into partnerships, you have to move through three specific stages: curiosity, courage, and conviction. First, be curious about how to integrate partnerships within your department, sales, marketing, and success teams. In my own career, I had held these positions and understood their needs, so I could influence them effectively. This background gave me the courage to push for the necessary changes. Finally, with conviction, you can confidently steer the company's direction and stake your reputation on these decisions."
>
> – Jared Fuller, Chief Partner and
> Ecosystem Officer, Reveal

Old Partnerships Versus New Partner Ecosystem Model

First, let's compare the old partnership model versus the new. In traditional Business-to-Business (B2B) partnership models, relationships tended to be transactional in nature. Partnerships were often formed with the main goal of achieving technical integrations or facilitating the closure of a gap in a sales cycle, typically focusing on short-term gains and immediate needs. The emphasis was often on sales volume, market share, and individual profit margins. As such, interactions between partners were centered on fulfilling specific transactions rather than building long-term collaborative relationships.

> "There's so much value, particularly when you're a startup or you're a smaller business, in getting really smart about how you participate in ecosystems."
> – Scott Brinker, VP Platform Ecosystem, HubSpot

The modern partner ecosystem model takes this outdated approach and flips it on its head. Instead, it takes a holistic approach to partnerships, in which both partners' attention is on creating value for the customer first and foremost. This model recognizes that customers are at the center of the business ecosystem and that delivering value to them is essential for sustained success. In a partner ecosystem, companies work together collaboratively, often across multiple organizations, to deliver comprehensive solutions for customers.

To do this, consultative and value-forward partner ecosystems prioritize understanding the customer's business objectives and challenges. Partners engage in consultative discussions with customers to identify their pain points and goals, and then work together to design solutions that meet those needs effectively. This approach requires a deeper level of investment in understanding customer industries, trends, and challenges.

The Hub-and-Spoke Model of Management

Although partners make your business better and improve your product offerings, it's important to know how to best manage as well as enable the partner in terms of forming a healthy and mutually beneficial relationship. This is where the hub-and-spoke model comes in, as shown in Figure 4.1.

Figure 4.1 The hub-and-spoke model.

Connect with other people who have worked with the same partners you're considering working with to get information that you won't get organically. Also, think through how you'll get feedback about a partner from your shared customers. This can't be left to chance; rather, it requires mechanisms to ensure you have insights into the partner's capabilities, reputation, and performance.

The more you develop a web of relationships around your partner, the stronger your partner relationship will be. It will influence how you do your quarterly business reviews and annual reviews, as well as how you measure customer happiness and what you record within your customer relationship management (CRM) system. It will extend to every single aspect of the business because, fundamentally, you're trying to get to a point where the partner is truly an extension of your team.

This means you'll be thinking about what they're working on as what you're working on. You'll think about their success in selling to a customer as a win for you and your team. They'll share information with you, and you'll conduct account-based marketing activities for your customer in conjunction with all of your different partners. You'll be marketing together, and it's a constant state of amplification when it's done right.

> "Traditionally, the way B2B growth happens is very lonely and isolated. When we try to grow a B2B company and we think about the way we sell and market, we're going to be unhappy and unsuccessful if we're doing it all alone. So why not find your tribe? People who want to win with you, in a way that is enlivening to the spirit. There's a lot of heart in this co-selling thing. It's not just about the mechanics."
>
> – Allan Adler, Managing Partner, Digital Bridge Partners

Setting Up Your Own Cheat Code

How do you set up your own Cheat Code? Justin alluded to it in Chapter 3, but partnerships are really about – and are in service of – the customer. At In Revenue Capital, we take a deep dive into the Ideal Partner Profile (IPP) when we evaluate a company for investment. The *Ideal Partner Profile* is similar to the *Ideal Customer Profile* (ICP) (see Figure 4.2), which you might already be familiar with, but if not, here is a quick recap.

Figure 4.2 The Ideal Partner Profile.

The ICP is a set of data points that represent the best-fit companies for your product or service. The output of most ICP exercises is a set of firmographic data points that represent the quantitative attributes of an ideal customer, paired with a set of more qualitative data points also representative of your best-fit customer.

In theory, an ICP customer should be the easiest to acquire with the highest retention and expansion potential relative to the rest of the addressable or serviceable market for your product or service. There are a host of tools and services out there now that can help you score accounts relative to your ICP criteria.

If you need help defining your ICP, you can download our ICP Toolkit by scanning the following QR code:

How to Set Up Your Own Cheat Code

Similarly, the IPP is a set of data points that represent the best-fit partners for your organization. The exercise and outputs are very similar to the ICP, but they can be a bit more nuanced in the qualitative metrics. Let's look at our IPP framework.

Firmographic Fit

Do you share the same ICP?

Scale of 1–10, 1 = no ICP crossover, 10 = identical ICP crossover

Ideal partners will have a very high ICP crossover. This should score at least an 8 for your initial set of partners.

Do you share the same buying center?

Scale of 1–10, 1 = completely different buying group, 10 = exact same buying group

Your IPP will sell into the same department as you, meaning if your solution is tailored to selling into marketing and the partner is tailored toward selling into human resources, this is a bad fit. Look for 7–10 as acceptable rankings in this category, because there are adjacent departments that can often act as interchangeable proxies for one another depending on the organization, such as marketing and sales.

Solution Fit

Do you fill a gap in the solution the potential partner offers to their customers?

Scale of 1–10, 1 = no, they have a similar solution, 10 = huge gap in their solution we fill

Think of objection handling. What objections do their sellers hear about their solution that you could solve with your solution?

Does your solution add quantifiable value to the joint customer?

Scale 1–10, 1 = zero value, 10 = amplifies value of partner

Think about working with your partner to build a business case for the joint solution. High scores should rank in this order:

- *8 – Offer independent quantifiable value*
- *9 – Add quantifiable value to their solution*
- *10 – Quantifiable amplification of partner value proposition; lower scores will show little to no or anecdotal value*

Culture Fit

It's worth noting that, if your score up to this point is less than 30, there's no reason to go further. This is clearly not a fit. If the score is above that, then continue on.

How does the potential partner view partners, and what have their previous experiences been?

Scale 1–10, 1 = don't have any, 10 = partners are a core growth lever

This scale should be tailored depending on what you are looking for in a partnership. If the company is new to partnership, it might be an uphill battle to get something meaningful off the ground. The other side of the spectrum could be equally as challenging, such as well-established, yet highly bureaucratic corporate partner programs. Those programs can be very mature and tough to crack. There are a variety of flavors in between, like partners who only do resell, or only have one-way referral partnerships. This leads directly to the next subset of qualification criteria:

What types of partnerships does this company currently have?

- *Resell*
- *Co-marketing*
- *Referral*
- *Co-sell*
- *Technology integration*

All can be good individually or collectively. We suggest scoring a point for each available.

How does the partner measure the success of a partnership?

- *Leads*
- *Sourced revenue*
- *Influenced revenue*
- *Partner attached (measured across all core Go-to-Market [GTM] metrics)*

We suggest assigning a scaled value to each based on what you are looking for in a partner.

Will this potential partner pilot the partnership with a customer?

Y/N

This is a critical piece of the equation. Most partnerships don't get off the ground because they start with formalities like partnership or referral agreements. If all of the other criteria have been met, the first step in taking action is starting with a customer. Ideally, both organizations have a customer to bring to the table to test and validate the solution. This is the absolute best way to gain momentum.

Some additional questions to consider:

- How is the potential partner already investing in partnerships, in terms of human capital and budget?
- Per Chapter 3, how aligned are executives to partner initiatives?
- In terms of the hub-and-spoke model we referenced, are you grading prospective partners based on other partners they're involved with?

This is roughly a 70-point framework that enables you to quantify your potential partnerships, saving you significant time and resources as you build toward being a partner-centric organization that integrates with your inbound and outbound efforts.

The IPP framework can be downloaded by scanning this QR code:

Additional Factors to Keep in Mind

Whether you are starting your partner program from scratch or have an established program in place, it's worth running all potential and current partners through this matrix to help you nail down where you should spend your time. Time is the most valuable resource in a startup. It can be very easy to go down rabbit holes with potential partners, so using this qualification criteria is a great way to help prioritize.

Thoughts from Cassandra Gholston

During Season Two of *The Cheat Code* podcast, we interviewed Cassandra Gholston, CEO of PartnerTap, the leading partner ecosystem and co-selling platform for the enterprise. She said it's imperative for founders to be thinking about the foundation of partnerships from day one. In the early days of PartnerTap, she needed to focus on the creation of a single strategic alliance – this is similar to the anecdote Jared Fuller shared in Chapter 3.

It was too much to build an entire partner ecosystem or tackle the enormity of a preestablished ecosystem; it was instead best to get narrow and focus on a single partner who maintained the closest proximity to her ideal customer. That meant for the first few years the business existed she focused on building a single very impactful partnership with software provider Impartner, who had a high degree of penetration into her desired customer base.

The focus on Impartner was the result of an exercise similar to the IPP exercise. The goal was to find the company with the closest proximity to the customers they wanted to sell to at PartnerTap. The key to forging that partnership was a give-to-get mentality. Cassandra shared a story with us about a trip to Dreamforce in 2017 (if you are unaware, Dreamforce is the user

---

conference for Salesforce.com and considered one of the – if not the – largest user conference in Software-as-a-Service).

From that conference, she started sending leads to sellers at Impartner. After sending a tranche of leads to the team, she reached out to the chief revenue officer at Impartner saying, "We just sent your sales team several leads. We have more to send your way and we are actively in the sales cycle with one of your top customers. I'd love to meet."

That focused, give-to-get approach kicked off what turned out to be their key GTM partner. Fast-forward seven years and PartnerTap was recognized as a top partner at their annual conference and has referred them their largest customers to date.

I cannot underscore the give-to-get mentality enough. Cassandra said, "When you are a smaller company expecting to partner with a bigger fish you should expect to give a lot before you will get anything in return."

"To understand a customer's ecosystem, identify what is already close to them – such as the tech, communities, and podcasts they engage with. As a company, you should connect the dots within this ecosystem, leveraging existing relationships to get closer to the customer. Instead of building a new ecosystem, integrate into the customer's existing one, which includes many of your partners. Some partners will align with your ideal profile, while others may not. The key is to understand the customer and their ecosystem, gaining proximity through trusted sources rather than through white papers, ebooks, webinars, cold calls, or interruptions." – Jill Rowley, GTM advisor and Limited Partner, Stage 2 Capital

51

How to Set Up Your Own Cheat Code

Moving forward, it really is all about the customer. Now that you have your ideal partner defined, the next critical piece is a deep understanding of where you fit at the intersection of the customer and the partner. We call this the *Joint Value Proposition (JVP)*.

The JVP is the value we bring to the customer together, as partners. It must be clear that there is differentiation between the individual customer value props of each organization. Setting up a JVP starts with looking at the gaps in your partners' solution, how your solution fills those gaps, and then creating a "better together" message.

The better together message needs to be as clear, concise, and as simple as the singular value prop or it will get lost. At LeadMD, "Fulfilling the promise of Marketing Automation" was a great example of a JVP. It clearly demonstrated the value of LeadMD *and* the dependency on marketing automation. It narrows our ICP and IPP in a singular statement. From there it's very easy to take that JVP and activate it with customers and partners.

This brings me to the final piece of the "getting started" puzzle. Field activation. Your Cheat Code does not work without this final piece. In fact, we spend significant time with you the rest of the way detailing how you activate your Cheat Code in the field. Spoiler alert . . . it all starts with relationships.

Everything we have covered to this point is to set the stage for field activation, which is literally canvasing your partner organization from top to bottom, building relationships that ultimately get you closer to the customer through a better together message built on a foundation of TRUST.

We continue to flesh out these concepts throughout the book, but for now a recap of how to set up your Cheat Code:

- Executive buy-in (see Chapter 3)
- ICP and IPP creation
- Give-to-get mentality
- JVP creation
- Field activation (Chapters 6–9)

This is just the beginning. Chapters 6–9 take deep dives into sales, marketing, customer success, and onboarding. Ultimately, these are the areas where relationships are forged in partnership. It's the best window into the customer and how to deliver on the promise of growth via partnership.

Chapter 5

Customer, Context, and Culture

Justin Gray

There are few absolutes in business, but for a partnership to work, you absolutely must check three mission-critical boxes that we'll coin *the three Cs*: customer, context, and culture. They simply must be in alignment between your company and any partnership you secure.

If the three Cs are not present and aligned, it's highly likely the partnership won't get very far off the ground in the first place. And even if it does, it will be doomed to the mediocrity that has predominately defined partner teams up until this point. Fundamentally, conflict between two partners within these aspects makes something that is already inherently hard even harder.

At the center of each of these tenets is the core shift from "me" to "we." Even the language of an organization is important to facilitating this mindset change. As Josh alluded to in Chapter 6, up until now, partners have been tapped largely to solve for an insurmountable problem. For example, the technology doesn't perform a key task the buyer is requesting, so they leverage a partner technology. Conversely, the prospect is interested in understanding implementation costs as part of the buying cycle, so they bring in a system integrator.

The point is that these are reactionary motions meant to quell an objection. Only when we've exhausted all possibilities to stand alone do we "complicate" our selling process by involving one of our so-called partners. And therein lies a window to an archaic mindset, which is rooted in failure.

The false narrative that persists in nearly every modern selling organization is the belief that adding more moving pieces will disrupt and lengthen the buying process. The funny thing is, anytime I've seen companies conduct studies into sales success and velocity, they've uncovered the opposite to be true. But more on this later. For now, we'll focus on a dataset that came about purely by accident but was so consistent in its findings we had to formalize the results into a framework, as shown in Figure 5.1.

Since early 2023, we've been running a podcast, the name of which you'll recognize if you're holding this book: *The Go-to-Market Cheat Code*. Our goal from the beginning was to speak to interesting people who were doing things in GTM unconventionally – essentially formulating their own cheat codes.

These conversations ultimately became the catalyst for this book because so many of them were based on this concept of relationships. At the same time, it was clear that leaders and teams had to blaze their own paths to success, because advisors and experts were touting playbooks (think inbound and outbound) that frankly no longer worked. As mentioned, there were some very obvious apex points of consistency – those similarities that ultimately became the three Cs.

The consistency with which executives across industries, annual contract value ranges, and even business models highlighted the need for these three Cs was in such a ubiquitous manner that we started to become very concerned for the potential monotony of our podcast content.

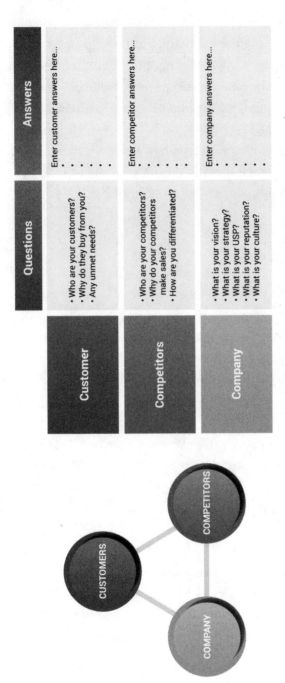

Figure 5.1 The three Cs of marketing framework. *Source:* Copyright In Review Capital.

But when something is so consistent among individuals who have been in the trenches of GTM and partnership programs for decades, it begs a deep dive. After digging in, it became clear that customer, context, and culture might comprise the ultimate checklist for determining success and failure when creating partner ecosystems.

To that end, this chapter dives into what we mean by the three Cs, and how to leverage them to ensure your organization is truly set up for success in the partner-led economy.

Customer

As with all things in business, we begin with the customer first, because it has to be the North Star on which success is plotted. As you start to determine your best partner opportunities, you need look no further than your ideal customer base. When evaluating the Go-to-Market (GTM) motions of our portfolio companies, it's always where we start.

Before you can effectively take a product or service to market, you first have to understand who needs it. Who finds value in it? In startups, there's rarely a straight line to success, but by starting with an Ideal Customer Profile definition, we have a starting point at least.

The same is true for designing and creating partner ecosystems and the programs that manage them. You begin at the beginning: with the customer. Simply put, true ecosystems develop when you fill them with partners who not only service the same ideal customer base but also the same buying centers and buyers within that base. We must serve the same master.

Curating Partners Based on Solution Overlap

Going even deeper, you want to work with partners who have strong solution overlap, meaning partners within the ecosystem provide solutions who all come together to solve for a core problem or need. We use the word *overlap* in a highly intentional way here because, by serving that problem or need for that same customer base, it's highly likely that you will also be solving the same elements of the same problem.

Relationships don't exist at the company level; you can't earn the trust of a faceless organization. You need to earn trust at the individual level. Only then can that relationship provide you the license to put a metaphorical arm around the shoulder of that buyer and usher in a partner who can help them.

We've all been a part of this process when it's done wrong. A situation in which, instead of that critical overlap, some sloppy seller attempts to use any open window into the company and then attempts to storm the castle. It looks like those random requests, often coming via channels like LinkedIn, where some eager folks attempt to leverage your connection within a company to gain entry for themselves.

The only problem, of course, is that your connection resides in a completely different functional area than their desired contact. It doesn't work – and it fails because relevancy is a really big factor. Simply because you once served the chief marketing officer of an organization does not mean the head of product cares about your relationship, and thus likely the same can be said of your solution. It seems obvious, and yet it happens all the time.

So, once you understand the profiles of your ideal customer and buying centers within those customers, that's where the ideal partner profiling exercise really takes off. With that knowledge, you should be digging into the goals of those buyers whom you influence. From there, it's not a big jump to identify others (e.g. potential ecosystem partners) who also influence those goals.

It's the age-old "better together" story in which the math of 1 plus 1 begins to equal 4, 8, or 12 even. Beginning with the customer and digging deep into that customer's jobs to be done (JTBD), and who can assist with those jobs, is one of those aspects of partnerships so agreed on it's a hardened rule. So, why then do so many partnership teams get off track?

At LeadMD, all of our customers were looking to solve for three fundamental problems: acquiring more customers, retaining more customers, and better using technology to do both. That's it. From our strategic partners down to our referral partners, they all focused on delivering or influencing those three fundamental needs. You can see the importance of knowing the exact problem your buyers have and also how exactly your solution addresses it, along with your potential gaps or shortcomings in doing so.

Of course, those gaps and shortcomings are exactly where you'll architect an ecosystem to extend your offering. Otherwise, things get messy really fast, and it's hard to even have the beginnings of a true partner conversation. Instead, they quickly devolve into simple referral conversations, or worse, a waste of time – and that's not what we're talking about when we say Cheat Code. Referrals can often give you a leg up, but they won't give you exponential scale overnight (which, in partner terms, still means 12–18 months).

As a consultancy and system integrator, we had the advantage of understanding our customer's core problems and goals, rather than superficial pains. In fact, we were often paid to find the true root of pains, the fundamental problem, and identify the right solutions. This provided us a comprehensive view, not only of the solution but also all of the necessary pieces to form that solution. The customer was going to need strategy, processes, people, and then, of course, technology.

Given that we could deliver all but the last piece, we built our partner ecosystem with the best-in-class technology partners necessary to automate, execute, and extend our services. Because the entire process was born from the customer, we knew those technology partners could enhance the experience we needed to deliver, but we also knew our services enhanced theirs. This created a true mutual value proposition, with the customer at the center.

Curating Partners Based on Customer Needs

"Partnerships are a surround strategy. Outbound calls and unsolicited emails are interruptions, which future customers dislike. Inbound marketing attracts customers by offering valuable content, conversations, and community engagement. Nearbound, which might become a new category, is a surround strategy that encompasses both inbound and outbound. The key is to think of concentric circles with the customer always at the center."

– Jill Rowley, GTM advisor and Limited Partner,
Stage 2 Capital

Even though all deals should ideally have a partner added to them, you must first know how to identify your customer's needs, pains, and use cases. Otherwise, you'll just be prematurely cramming the

61

need for partners down someone's throat. That's not only ineffective, but also potentially alienating.

For example, maybe a customer is struggling with their ability to convert inbound interest through their website into viable sales opportunities. A clear-cut case for some shiny new software, right? Maybe a predictive insights solution at that, one that provides visibility into all of the digital footprints they've left across the web. However, on digging deeper you find they actually already have access to a tool, which the former CMO purchased before leaving last fall, and it does just that. What began as an apparent gap in technology was actually a lack of software adoption. This would be an excellent use case for bringing in a services partner or a training partner. Understanding not just the pain, but the root problem, will help ensure that the partnerships you activate yield true strategic value to all involved. It's easy to fall into the allure of delivering a high volume of leads to partners, but unless that referral delivers the right kind of results, you put several important relationships at risk.

Tip: Businesses would be wise to build out their partner ecosystem based on core customer needs and problems. If you take the time to identify the value propositions of each one of those types of partners – and even individual partners themselves – you'll become more adept at discovering client needs and matching the right partners to them.

Context

Although insight into the customer is the foundational building block of any successful partner ecosystem, that knowledge can't be translated into action without context. A McKinsey poll of global executives reported that 84% of leaders identified that innovation was extremely important to their growth strategies, but a staggering 94% were dissatisfied with their organizations' innovation performance.[1] Why the disconnect?

Something as innovative to modern GTM strategies as partner ecosystems succeeds only when we translate customer needs into the solution created through partnerships. And yet, that context so often gets lost in favor of technical features or superficial marketing speak that doesn't convey value.

The Jobs-to-Be-Done Framework

There's a great framework called JTBD, which was developed by Tony Ulwick, the founder of the innovation consulting firm called Strategyn. The concept behind JTBD combats a fallacy that happens far too often in GTM in general, and it is pervasive in nearly every partnership program I've seen fail.

In partnerships, the trend is to define a "product." That productization-centric thinking enables teams to easily consume when and where to engage a partner. Of course, we know the answer to that question is "every time" and "everywhere" if you're truly adopting a partnership mentality, and we'll dive deeper into that in the Culture section. But historically, partnerships have been viewed through the lens of desperation. Only when we can no longer go it alone do we go together.

Therefore, when attempting to define those unconquerable barriers, teams turn to this easy-to-consume "product" mentality. You've no doubt seen this in practice. "I need a health care partner who

Customer, Context, and Culture

performs customer relationship management (CRM) implementations" or "I need to know who our go-to partner is for secure file transfer in manufacturing."

Although these well-defined, and often pain-based, products can be attractive when attempting to get teams to self-prescribe partner involvement, they're woefully reactive and, most important, they don't serve the customer's true needs. This is where JTBD becomes incredibly effective because it seeks to frame customer needs through their own language and, in fact, their own headspace.

Fundamentally, what are the core jobs that customers go to sleep and wake up thinking about? Only when we truly put ourselves in the shoes of our customers and walk that mile in service of the needs that get them promoted or fired can we truly architect an ecosystem-led solution. We have to pivot into the proactive architecture of value-based solutions, rather than reactive and cobbled together bandages that solve only for superficial pains.

The difference between organizations whose understanding of the customer extends only to the boardroom and an ethereal strategy versus those who translate that understanding to the field in a way that taps into the buyer's mindset (as well as activates trust through a curated partner approach in service of that mindset) is a fundamental understanding of the customer's JTBD. See Figure 5.2.

We've deployed this helpful tool at many of our past clients and portfolio companies, but perhaps the best implementation of it that I've seen was through a process we created at LeadMD.

The customer evaluation exercise helped us find the potential partners who served the same customers that we served, and whose

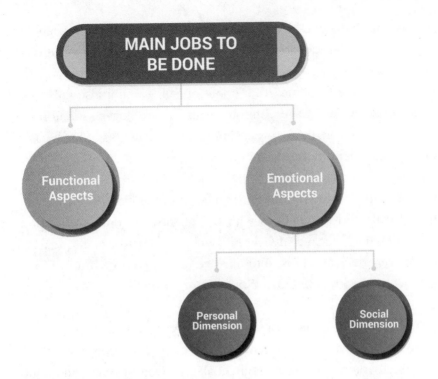

Figure 5.2 The jobs-to-be-done framework. *Source:* Copyright In Review Capital.

solutions served the same customer needs. It also helped us define partners who could assist us in delivering our value – truly homogenous. That's an important concept.

Achieving Meaningful Outcomes

Now, as they say, the devil is in the details. Or, in this case, the operationalization of this context is in the details. It's not uncommon for context to exist and then quickly dissipate when action is required across the nuanced mechanisms and the inner workings of a company.

This is the "whack-a-mole" game that today's partner managers play, running from department to contact within their organizations attempting to align everyone on a partner opportunity they have uncovered at the frontline. It's a noble pursuit – and it also fails. We implemented what I have come to realize is an elegant solution to this problem. At the time, it was simply a pragmatic way to solve for a serious problem in the business.

As a marketing agency, our consultants spent the better part of their day on calls and in meetings with our clients. These conversations were of course critical to delivering value, but what I came to realize is they were also a window into massive untapped opportunity – not only for our product but also those of our partners.

This is the great benefit of a services organization. Once you've earned customer trust, they will share more problems with you. They'll tell you about the strategic goals they were concerned about achieving – gaps in talent within the organization and the tools and technology they were struggling with or considering purchasing.

It was a sales professional's dream. Of course, the key was that they weren't having these conversations with sales. Had we attempted to interject sales into that process, our clients would have clammed up quickly – and rightly so. No one wants to be sold to; they want help from people they trust.

We had long since tried to incentivize our consultants to identify opportunities to involve our partners. After all, the purchase of more technology required more services to implement them and ensure they worked. But this felt foreign to many of our consultants when we attempted to place the responsibility of referring partners on their shoulders. They don't want to be seen as "pitching" and, therefore, the seemingly initiative solution produced somewhat lukewarm results. Something needed to change.

One day I started to think about what truly drove the sale of new projects and how our clients thought about those projects. When we were really successful in our clients' eyes, we weren't delivering, well, deliverables. We were helping them achieve big outcomes.

We weren't simply helping them implement ABC technology or create XYZ campaigns, but we were helping them achieve big, meaningful shifts. Shifts like "help us drive 30% more revenue through marketing" or "help us successfully launch this new product and drive $10 million in bookings in the first half of the year." Those were "big O" outcomes.

They were also broad in nature, which enabled us often to architect an entire supporting technology stack that would be necessary or, at the very least, pieces of that stack. These were the types of projects where we could truly activate our partner ecosystem and deliver on those hyper-valuable joint value propositions (JVPs).

If we could figure out a way to capture the "big O" outcomes our clients were sharing with our consulting teams almost daily, we could drive value for ourselves, our partners, and our customers, all in one. On top of this, it also solved the conundrum every small to medium-sized services business faces, which is the ability to drive reciprocity to its partners.

Our technology partners were large technology providers, with deep war chests and big brands. In other words, they were experts at driving demand for their product and we were asking them to involve us in those deals, above their other partners that were competitive

Customer, Context, and Culture

with us. The friction there, of course, is that they'd need to know what we were going to bring to them in return. Yes, successful customers might feel like a great answer, but it wasn't an acceptable one. These large providers were looking for revenue impact – and this process could deliver on that differentiator.

So, we went to work. We re-architected our entire lead life cycle around an entry point that was no longer lead-based but, you guessed it, outcome-based. An outcome was now the first step in our sales process. The presence of a right-fit customer account and buyer were table stakes, but in order to begin the process of selling, we had to understand what the prospect was looking to achieve and how they would measure it.

We created a new custom object in our CRM to support this, which not only captured the critical dimensions of what we determined to be an outcome – needs, pains, necessary deliverables, success metrics, and the whole nine yards – but also each outcome could also accommodate one or more partners, and the underlying reasons why those partners were necessary.

Finally, they could move in a fluid manner through the qualification process and the sales process (what many people think of as opportunities) and then ultimately were associated with the project that resulted from the sale. In this way, we could ensure that the fundamental goals of the customer were never overlooked across the entire life cycle.

Even more to the point, we could determine the success of our deliverables against the client's successful achievement of their true strategic goals. Projects didn't just become completed based on a checklist; they were complete when the client had hit their definition of success. This was a game changer.

We then set about aligning our internal talent management and coaching processes in service of outcomes. We implemented targets for each role and by team. The goal was understanding how many problems and potential solutions our consultants could uncover within their client base.

That was the edict from the top and reinforced by team leaders. We created dashboards that would highlight individual and team performance and how it was improving over time. But perhaps most critically, we aligned compensation and rewards to the actions we wanted to see.

All partners pay referral fees – it's a known standard. But where do those reward monies go? At most organizations, who knows? Well, at LeadMD, in the case where a created outcome resulted in a successful sale, 25% of that referral spiff went to the consultant who had created the outcome, 50% went to the seller, and 25% stayed at the house.

These referral fees were not small change, considering that 25% of a typical referral could be $5000, $10 000, or $15 000 easily. These were meaningful rewards for performing a process that was absolutely critical in preserving the context necessary to successfully activate the partner ecosystem on which our very business relied.

We now had a mechanism to capture the insights our clients were sharing with our teams, and in a way that avoided saddling them with sales responsibilities. Each time an outcome was created for a prospect or client, it was routed to the appropriate sales team, either new business or existing client expansion.

There, it was curated and taken through an intense qualification process where the outcome was often refined by involving other executives within the buying committee until we had a true understanding of not only a pain, but a true mission-critical initiative worthy of investment. This deep understanding is a hunting license, because once a client truly believes you understand their business and needs, they trust you to involve other parties in service of those goals.

Culture

Now on to the big one: culture. Let's face it. You can do everything in this book but if your organization doesn't live and breathe a partnership mindset, you're going to fail. We alluded to this previously. But to reiterate, it was eerie how well aligned the dozens and dozens of partner executives we've spoken to on our podcast were in their belief in these three Cs – and in the fact that partnerships, like culture, are fundamentally led from the top down. This is to say that if your CEO doesn't see the inherent value in partner ecosystems, it's an uphill battle all along the way.

I coach a lot of marketers in their career, simply because I used to employ troves of marketing consultants, and undoubtedly one of the questions I receive is, "What if the CEO doesn't believe in marketing?" My answer is, without fail, "Don't work there."

Now, given that partner ecosystems are undergoing a spring of sorts, largely because of the inbound and outbound ineffectiveness we talked about in the first chapter, I would give CEOs a bit of grace in terms of a learning curve when it comes to partner mentality and cultural support for its effectiveness – but only a bit.

The fact is partner mentality runs counter to the overnight results mentality that many CEOs still fall back on. Partnerships require time and effort and, without support from the top, those necessary ingredients are naturally going to be in short supply.

Due to the slowdown across the board in Business-to-Business demand these days, the fortunate tailwind in the market is that most CEOs are willing to give new strategies some oxygen, and herein lies the opportunity. But the problem is, when given the chance, most revenue executives don't know how to execute it, simply because they've never seen it done before. So, here's how we did it.

Culture is built on beliefs, and nothing facilitates belief better than powerful stories. Whenever we are attempting to determine both partner fit as well as the adoption of that partner fit internally, we have to begin with the establishment of an incredibly strong JVP.

The Partnership with Marketo

When we first approached Marketo about a partnership with LeadMD, they essentially told us to kick rocks. Implementation and enablement services provided by a consultancy outside their walls ran counter to their brand at the time. Remember, their core message in the early days was that using their platform was "easy." Having us involved and needed by the client implied this whole thing was not so easy.

But, once Marketo became open to partnerships culturally, we were no longer viewed as a spoil to their brand message but a deliverer of it. The JVP was simple – we were what made Marketo easy. Of course, it's worth noting that this came on the heels of incredibly high churn, which is what ultimately opened their eyes to the need for services partners. But this is why partnerships take time and investment.

The motivator that kept us focused on pursuing a partnership in those early days was our direct client insight. We had used Marketo, and we had also spoken to a lot of other users before starting the business. We knew that Marketo wasn't easy. Well, let me caveat that – the actual Marketo software was incredibly easy, with beautiful, simple, drag-and-drop features that enabled powerful marketing tactics.

However, the problem was most of what fueled Marketo, the processes and tactics it automated, were in fact very new to marketers, and that introduced the difficulty. They had never scored and segmented and nurtured and even executed comprehensive digital campaigns, because it wasn't possible prior to the marketing automation wave that Marketo helped to usher. The software was new, and the software enabled all of these new tactics that have now become commonplace. But in those days, marketers needed help. We knew this and therefore we kept at it.

Not only did we make a relatively easy platform easier, but most essential for Marketo was our ability to remedy the hesitation many organizations had about finding talent to manage this new platform once they had acquired it. We were teachers and catalysts of change within a rapidly transitioning marketing function so we could also be a necessary bridge enabling an organization to use the technology right out of the gate, even while they searched for a long-term solution to its daily administration.

This ability to help customers extract immediate and reliable value from marketing automation in turn had a measurable impact on churn reduction. As such, Marketo began to see the contextual gaps we were finding and filling, culturally, so then they began to see the value of partnerships – at least at the executive level.

This is where most partnerships begin, and also end. The act of securing a partnership is in no way the guarantee of its success. That success is fostered in the field, by the frontline sellers responsible for customer acquisition and also the backend teams responsible for ensuring those customers' success with the platform.

Fortunately, these are also the points where we as the partner extract the most value. Therefore, from day one of the partnership we embedded ourselves in Marketo's San Mateo offices. So much in fact that over the coming weeks and months it was common for their employees to believe we actually worked there. Due to that proximity, we were able to rapidly understand things like prospect objections and customer pains and in turn augment those sellers and conversations with remedies we could provide.

This is the investment level that true strategic partnerships require. For years, our charge was indoctrinating Marketo's employees – forming real relationships with as many individuals as possible and fostering top-of-mind awareness for our organization and our services.

This required not just warm bodies based in California but threaded support and aircover from other functions within LeadMD, including marketing, executives, and our consulting teams. Everyone across our organization was greeted with a partner-first message from the moment they joined our organization, and the supporting motions in service of it were integrated into their career path, compensation, and coaching. For almost three years I boarded a plane every two weeks to fly from my home in Arizona to my apartment in San Francisco. From that perch in the tendernob (the intersection between the upper-class neighborhood of Nob Hill and the down-trodden Tenderloin), I ran both the company as well as our sales team, who were also based in the Bay Area.

Now, this wasn't only due to Marketo – we had many other partners near the same area – but Marketo was the most critical because our solutions were so fundamentally aligned. You didn't embrace digital marketing transformation without a marketing automation software; you just didn't. You also didn't invest in the software component, without exploring implementation and support options. Because of this degree of market alignment, as well as obvious executive investment, it was easy for my teams to understand where our priorities were and mirror the same behaviors and focus.

This yielded such indisputable results, we began to run these same playbooks with other partners we wanted to develop. Our sales became integrated into everything about our chosen partners, right down to their sales contests. We advertised not only the successful referrals from their account executives and customer success managers but also ensured their peers could see why and how we were rewarding them. Their annual top performers, "president's trips" were augmented by our own piggybacked excursions, designed specifically to highlight those individuals who had opened the doors for our sales efforts. We rewarded these top performers with trips to Napa, Lake Tahoe, and even Lollapalooza in Chicago to foster aspiration among teammates.

Email newsletters and physical leave-behinds told the stories of large deals we had won together, their sellers leveraging our team to overcome objections and foster adoption they could not have achieved on their own. Similarly, we would not have gained our access to customers had it not been for them – a highly functioning ecosystem to say the least.

We presented at their sales kick-off meetings and hosted lunch-and-learns based not on services and who we were, as is common, but on real stories of collaboration and success between our teams. We earned the right to ensure this was always in motion both by being present and then ensuring the payoff was real, tangible value at the human level.

From roughly 2011 to 2018, if you purchased Marketo, there was a 30% chance we did your implementation. In the last three years, that ratio also included internal professional services they sold on their paper, as we had begun performing true white-label service delivery for their internal teams.

From those early years up until our acquisition in February 2021, we performed almost 4000 Marketo implementations. This is not a normal growth story for a boutique consultancy based in Scottsdale, Arizona – and yet the most abnormal aspect was our relentless focus on partner-led growth, which spanned over a decade and also permeated every level of our two organizations.

Customer, Context, and Culture in a Portfolio Company

These days when we design similar programs for our portfolio investments, yes, we leverage these stories for context. It's always good to relive the good old days, but we're also quick to ensure these stories don't remain as such as we begin work by identifying potential partners where a similar and honest JVP exists. There's no way to fake value. There's no way to sidestep that fundamental seed from which all other aspects of partner success grow.

Once identified, we assemble a JVP that has branches from it that we can permeate into each team inside that organization. Of course, just like the LeadMD story, those team messages will eventually become individualized down to the human level as relationships form. This tree of value is what made the LeadMD program not only successful but also cultural.

One of our smaller seed stage investments is a company called Pitstop. They're an AI-powered predictive intelligence solution for large fleets of vehicles. Their insights reduce vehicle downtime (something every fleet wants to avoid), based on huge sets of data, but one data source that must always be present comes from a pervasive technology in their industry called *telematics*.

Telematics broadcasts data from the vehicles it is installed within so that fleet managers can see what's happening with their vehicles in real time. But telematics is reactive. It shows what *has* already happened. In a nutshell, Pitstop is proactive. It can tell any company with a fleet of trucks or cars what *will* happen, including how soon those vehicles will need repair and, equally as important, what repairs to prioritize.

If we apply the three Cs triangle to their world, it looks like this: (1) customer: large fleets, (2) context: downtime, (3) culture: provide insights. All three of those aspects benefit from Pitstop. Without Pitstop, the fleet manager is responsible for trying to construct an impossible crystal ball of insight; they have data from their trucks but really no idea how that data translates to future performance. It's yesterday's, last week's or last month's data, not what is happening now. It's the equivalent of trying to understand tomorrows weather based on a newspaper from three weeks ago. See Figure 5.3.

Fleet managers add Pitstop, which makes sense of the data, and suddenly, they can predict that a particular truck will break down in two months. So, while changing the tires that week, they can perform two

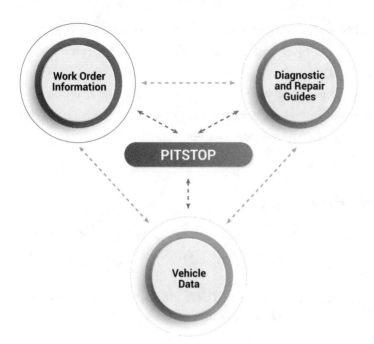

Figure 5.3 The Pitstop triangle. *Source:* Copyright In Review Capital.

other services proactively in order to avoid taking that truck off the road in the future. Subsequently, Pitstop is solving a big problem for the customer – loss of revenue due to fleet downtime – and similarly they are also solving a problem for the sellers and success teams inside of telematics and fleet management solutions by augmenting their solution's ability to not only look back but also look ahead.

The biggest objections fleet management software sellers and telematics providers in the space receive is "so what?" It's another source of data without insight into what to do next. We can help them overcome that objection and ensure their solutions provide value above and beyond their competition. When we tailor our value propositions for each of the key player's JTBD, we become a vital part of that job.

You're probably seeing where this is headed. Now, you can participate in every sale, not just within one of these providers, but in every fleet management and telematics technology provider in the space. That translates to a lucrative, force-multiplying pipeline. Once you agree on the customer and context match, you can permeate the culture, which can be the biggest challenge of the three.

More Than Just Referrals

As discussed previously in Chapter 5, you're going to get people who, after hearing your pitch, will say, "Great. You send us referrals, and we'll send you referrals." That's a legacy bias and firmly not what partner ecosystems are truly about. That's leaving a lot of opportunity on the table. The idea is to shift from a superficial sales/compensation culture to a better together culture. It's walking in as a complete solution that eliminates a significant joint customer problem.

If the company can grasp that culturally, then you're golden. If they're finding it difficult, it's usually based on fear – fear of losing control of the sale, primarily. The company might also want to strike a licensing arrangement. That's not a bad partnership option: 1 plus 1 equals 2. But when you can unite to win where each partner brings more than simply the sum of their parts, 1 plus 1 can equal 10 or more for everyone.

The best partnerships are those where the partners depend on each other. Do you make me better? Do I make you better? Those are the kind of questions you need positive answers to. So, in Pitstop's case, customers need telematics for the fleet information to flow. And what good is telematics if you don't know what to do with the information?

Customers need fleet management and maintenance providers to manage and maintain their assets. That's not nearly as valuable if those customers don't know what to do with the information and get too many unplanned maintenance breakdowns. What's missing is the one thing that pulls it all together – predictability. Everything and everyone gets smarter, more efficient, and more profitable. Everyone makes everyone better, and the customer wins.

Final Thoughts on Customer, Context, and Culture

All too often, unseasoned partnership teams think that once they get this kind of buy-in, they are on to something and have scored a hit. But unless they have made their way high up the corporate ladder and low down to the field teams, as well as have achieved customer, context, and cultural matches, they have a long way to go.

As you can see, the three boxes of customer, context, and culture take time and effort to complete. If they are easy, you have not gone high, deep, or wide enough. One way to find out if you have a match is simply to attempt a co-selling process together. Do a test run before any paperwork crosses the CEO's desk. Let's get a boat in the water and prove the hypothesis: yes, we make each other better.

"Unlike traditional channel partnerships, there's no need for exclusive agreements. Instead, collaborate on small projects, earn each other's respect, and experiment quickly."
– Chris Samila, cofounder and Chief Partner Officer, Partnership Leaders

When you can agree on a test case, be sure that the test case is with a relationship you already have. Too often, in a moment of "Let's do this!" energy, you agree to find a "mutual prospect" in order to validate the partnership. That is the worst thing that you can ever do because there are so many things that could stop the program in its tracks before it even gets under way, like agreeing on the customer. Or whose customer it should be. So, please, test it out in safe waters.

Ideally, this proof point is a trusted relationship who can open the door to honest conversation. You don't need to build a whole marketing campaign, find a new joint prospect, or assemble an army of people to test the hypothesis. That's unnecessary, expensive, and very ineffective.

Instead, think of it this way: "Do you want to meet one of my best customers?" When you can create a strong use case through a single willing test customer, and the experiment works, with honest ROI attached, you have developed a joint customer story that the company and its teams can rally around. That's how you check a lot of boxes.

Chapter 6

Partner Ecosystem
Nuts and Bolts

Josh Wagner

In Chapter 5, Justin poured us a solid foundation of customer, context, and culture. Next, we take a deep dive into the nuts and bolts of building out your partner ecosystem, mostly through the lens of context.

Justin talked about how, at LeadMD, we used outcomes as the impetus behind the context for serving a customer in the most impactful way. That took shape in a variety of different ways. Outcomes were a view into what success looked like through the eyes of the customer. It was our job on the frontlines – we made this a sales function – to parse through outcomes and use them as triggers for deeper conversations.

As Justin mentioned, consultants often did not want to be "selling" for fear of losing their objective trust with the customer. Although our sales team was incredibly consultative, the expectation was certainly that we would sell. Our customers knew this as well, but outcomes became valuable insight for very impactful sales conversations – conversations we could use to sell more of our services as well as tee up use cases, which also involved our partners.

Those use cases enabled us to work with those partners to help them engineer opportunities rooted in business impact. This was a far cry from the feature/function sales cycles you see from most Software-as-a-Service account executives out there. This was good for the customer and good for the partner.

> "I would even argue that, at the highest level, what [partner] ecosystems are really all about is transforming business for good."
> – Allan Adler, Managing Partner, Digital Bridge Partners

Again, all three ingredients outlined in the prior chapter are present here. We had proximity to the customer, we gained context through outcomes, and our culture was one that ensured partnerships were threaded throughout. It didn't just live with Justin, or even Justin and the sales department. It was top to bottom, left to right, embedded throughout the organization.

We are all familiar with the traditional sales funnel, or maybe more recently the revenue bow tie model, or perhaps one of the many iterations of those models intended to showcase the full customer life cycle, as shown in Figure 6.1.

The next evolution of those life cycle models needs to include a method of integrating partners in the same fundamental way we saw at LeadMD. The partner ecosystem methodology, shown in Figure 6.2, layers the context of relationships throughout all key Go-to-Market (GTM) functions of the organization. The most common outcomes we uncovered with our customers were related to acquiring and/or retaining customers. Those outcomes become the top of the model because they represent the customer use cases we are trying to solve.

Figure 6.1 Examples of the traditional and bow tie sales funnel. *Source:* Copyright In Review Capital.

Using that customer context, we immediately tap into the partner layer as a proxy for trust. That spreads across all GTM functions – inbound, outbound, onboarding, and customer success. That's right: inbound and outbound still have a place in the new GTM play-book, but the addition of "trust" is what enables them to function in the new world. That way, there is the best chance of capturing customer context, through the lens of established relationships and then leveraging it in to perpetuate a healthy ecosystem.

Again, we built a culture on partnerships that this was not just a sales function or a marketing function; this was a company function.

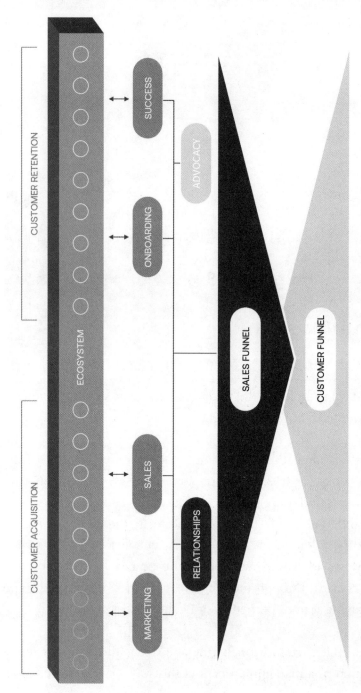

Figure 6.2 The Partner Ecosystem Methodology. *Source:* Copyright In Review Capital.

The Go-to-Market Cheat Code

We had to align our entire business throughout the entire business of our partners. That way, those relationships could organically turn into impact-based sales opportunities for us and every partner in the ecosystem.

Because this is not your typical GTM framework or funnel, you cannot rely on or expect your partners to have this type of framework in place; it's up to you to build this structure and to weave the partner into everything that touches the customer. The following sections look at how we built this model into the fabric over every function at LeadMD and wove it into the fabric of our relationships in the field with Marketo.

Inbound (Marketing)

Inbound is a function led by marketing and picked up by sales. Marketo was an inbound machine, especially in the early days. They were producing content at an unprecedented clip, and it was driving the marketing automation movement in the market. As a partner, we both benefited from, and contributed to, that content machine. The rising tide lifted all boats. They were in category-creation mode, backed by enormous financing, and there was no way we could match their output, but we were the beneficiaries both directly and indirectly simply by ensuring partners had a crucial role in the machine.

Our contributions to the machine were not insignificant. We believed in the power of marketing at LeadMD. The content we produced was aimed at solving some of the most common challenges the customer had with the software. Our front row seat as a top consulting and implementation partner gave us insight and authority. We knew firsthand what the customer was thinking, feeling, and experiencing daily and even hourly.

As such, we were able to leverage that deep understanding to create our own content, which fed the inbound machine and opened more doors for LeadMD and Marketo. Additionally, our perspective was frequently used in joint marketing content with Marketo like ebooks, blogs, and webinars to showcase depth and breadth of expertise and, most important, showcase the customer and their successes.

We've talked a lot about partnerships not just being about referrals, but let's be honest: partner-sourced leads are easy to measure and executives love the metric. Our proximity to Marketo and our own inbound machine enabled us to be the number one referral partner for sourced deals several years in a row. This was not an easy feat, especially when you're in the arena with much larger players, including some of the huge management consulting firms that later got into the marketing automation game.

Outbound (Sales)

As our solution set grew from simply Marketo-centric services, and Marketo began to "hit a ceiling" with inbound, there was a natural move within both organizations to rely more on sales-led outbound. There is no way to sugarcoat it; outbound is hard, and going outbound with a professional services or consulting solution is even harder. It's not tangible, there is nothing to demo; it's simply selling the solutions to problems. That's exactly what made outbound framed as a trusted Marketo partner a game we could win. Because it wasn't common for service partners to have a dedicated sales team, we coupled traditional sales methods with a consulting approach to tilt the scale in our favor.

The focus of our outbound efforts at LeadMD were centered on two themes we devised and tested, "twisting the knife" and "predicting the future." We didn't have an army of sellers; we were a small very strategic team and had to be incredibly focused in our efforts. Because our product was people, and those resources were solely focused on making the promise of marketing automation a reality, we had access to deep insights that revealed what customers were actually struggling with on the platform. As a sales team, we worked closely with our marketing department to extract insights from our consulting team. This type of close collaboration led to the development of a "Marketo maturity model" focused on the results a Marketo customer should expect as a natural progression of platform maturity. We used that model as the fuel for our outbound efforts because the biggest question among customers turned out to be, "are we getting the value from the platform we should be and how do we stack up against our peers?"

To complement our efforts, we leveraged tools that provided insight into the technographic footprint of companies, and those tools enabled us to target companies that had not only purchased Marketo but also specifically when they had added the Marketo tracking pixel to their website. The time component of the tracking pixel install was huge because it enabled us to prospect based on a strong proxy for their purchase date and align to that an assumed level of maturity.

Each outbound call, email, and social media outreach was meant to predict the future based on where we knew they were in their journey and based on the assumed starting point derived from the tracking pixel data we collected. We were rarely wrong and built a tremendous pipeline as a result. Interestingly, we once had a prospect reply to an email telling us that based on our prediction they were going to prove us wrong and do it on their own . . . six months later they came back saying we were right and signed up for a consulting engagement to get them up to the appropriate maturity level.

Onboarding (Customer Success and Professional Services)

Implementation was a big topic at Marketo. Although Marketo was technically "easy" to implement, it wasn't easy from a functional perspective. Every company who purchased Marketo bought it for the functionality, not for the technical implementation. Success for Marketo's implementation team (internal professional services) was technical implementation, meaning if the functional components of the platform technically worked, their work was done. Functional application of the technology was not within their purview or expertise.

Conceptually, they were sold the dream, and we made it our job to bring the dream to life. We had to dive deep into use cases, internal processes that supported those use cases, limitations, blockers, politics – you name it, we dealt with it. As a strategic partner, we had the ability to focus on what a successful implementation looked like as defined by the customer, not limited to the achievement of technical plumbing and wiring Marketo was using to define the end of their onboarding.

During that time, Marketo customers who implemented with a partner (not just LeadMD) were 70%+ more likely to renew than those who did not. Beyond that, their lifetime value was 35% higher, and they were more likely to have four or more integrations leveraging other ecosystem partners, which made the platform exponentially stickier.

That's perhaps the best illustration I've seen for why partners are so critical, and it's also a great example of the types of business impact a high-functioning partner ecosystem can have.

Customer Success (Consulting and Professional Services)

The LeadMD team was the ultimate Cheat Code for the Customer Success Team at Marketo. As the customer service hub for a rapidly scaling software darling, the team typically managed dozens, even hundreds, of accounts per customer success representative. Not only was this unmanageable but it also ensured that customer success managers (CSMs) were unable to focus on anyone but the most "at-risk" customers.

This neglected a large swath of client accounts in the middle, which meant they were a bubbling caldron of churn potential with little to no engagement by the CSM until the time came to execute a renewal contract. However, CSMs who leveraged LeadMD enjoyed above-average renewal rates and were more successful at cross-selling and upselling than those who did not.

That took a variety of forms. If we did the implementation, it was an easy handoff to our consulting team to support the client through one of our managed services offerings. However, if we didn't do the initial setup, introducing a partner could be a tricky situation for the Marketo team. The best customer success folks worked directly with the leaders on our consulting team, asking them for knowledge they could deploy in opportunistic situations and adding it to their own personal arsenal. We used those opportunities to uncover more outcomes that would be used in future sales efforts.

But they also looked for strategic entry points to leverage our team when client inquiries required deep expertise. Our consultants were our product, so a product demo often took the shape of solving a very acute problem, for free. If we were able to leverage this and provide access to our people in a very strategic way, we knew we could convert them to a customer based on providing them with a highly valuable experience. The Customer Success Team at Marketo was that strategic entry point that enabled us to identify accounts that needed help and then knock their socks off with the insights our team could provide when they needed them most.

The nuts and bolts of the Cheat Code look like the mapping of GTM functions across each partner organization. The Joint Value Proposition (JVP) based on the customer and then amplified by culture creates consistency at every level of the organization. How do you as a partner make their life better? For LeadMD, fulfilling the promise of marketing automation was the customer JVP, but at each go to market function within those walls, activation of that JVP meant something slightly different as we uncovered the pains of each individual counterpart and then solved for them.

> "A partner ecosystem acts as a force multiplier. Instead of having a small sales team, leveraging a larger network amplifies your reach and impact. It's about tapping into bigger organizations to drive growth and success."
> – Lauren Goldstein, General Manager, growth equity and private equity business, Winning by Design

The next few chapters take a deep dive into each of these functions and explain how we coach the companies in our portfolio to activate partnerships once the nuts and bolts are in place.

Chapter 7

Co-Marketing

Justin Gray

Now the rubber meets the road. It's time to put all of this into action. When operationalizing a new partner relationship, the most important thing to remember is to make every step actionable. We can't emphasize that enough.

Often, when exploring partnership opportunities, the conversations quickly become idealistic brainstorming sessions about who you both can help together, what you can help them do, how much it will increase revenue, and so forth. Although seemingly intuitive and even fun, this will get you nowhere. What will get you somewhere is keeping action as the primary focus.

> **Tip:** The first piece of advice – and it's a biggie – is that the most actionable thing you can do is start with a live use case. That means one or both of you must bring a customer to the table. Your partnership will never get off the ground by mutually finding a "net new" prospect together.

Introducing a Partner Solution

This book refers to the Cheat Code for a reason. It's a shortcut, and the way you unlock that shortcut is typically in the form of trust.

You've heard that word throughout this book. Trust, or lack thereof, will present itself when you look at your existing book of business with an open mind and ask yourself these questions, with the goal of identifying partner potential:

- Does the customer suffer a pain that can be solved from the value of our joint solution?
- Do we have this customer's trust to bring them new ideas?
- Is this customer typically open to new ideas?
- Does this customer have the budget flexibility and/or spend autonomy to pilot new ideas?
- Will this customer provide open and honest feedback about the new joint solution?
- Will this customer stick with us, should this pilot fail?

Most of us have a stable of "best customers." Start there and answer these questions as objectively as possible for each. Ideally, you and your new partner will be able to narrow the search down to at least one customer each, putting into play immediate reciprocity, which in and of itself builds trust. The other benefit produced by both you and your partner identifying this "beta" opportunity to mutually approach is that you get feedback on the joint solution from both angles.

Note: Tactically, the person who has established the most trusted relationship with the customer is the one who takes the initiative first. Sounds pretty obvious, but we can't tell you how often this comes as a surprise and how often egos or possessiveness can get in the way. In terms of the actual approach and outreach, this too should be spearheaded by the individual with the deepest relationship. This can be an executive, a customer success representative, or an account executive (AE), regardless of where the actual customer management responsibility currently sits in your organization. Don't let process get in the way of pragmatism.

Again, the Cheat Code or the "shortcut" is based on trust that has already been built. Once you use that as your foundation, set a meeting that includes the customer and your new partner. When you make the appointment, be honest about what is going to happen (e.g. that you are making an introduction into a sales cycle). Tee it up the right way to avoid the customer feeling blindsided.

Introducing a partner solution to a customer the first time can be scary, so be direct and succinct. You can use the following as a basis, and adjust as you see fit:

> We're evaluating a new partner squarely focused on (solving customer churn). I remember we talked about (that) in our last business review meeting. I've been thinking about how to help you with (that). Do you mind if I make an introduction so we can evaluate if (they) are a fit for you?

Such an introduction builds on the existing trust you have with the customer, reminds them that you are listening and actively looking to help them solve problems both inside as well as outside of your own solution set, and it prepares your partner for success in delivering a solution to a known problem. Remember, this partnership should not exist if your partner is not solving a common problem you run into with your customers.

Once you've made the introduction, it's now up to your new partner to run a high-value sales cycle. We talk about this specifically later in the book but, for our purposes here, understand that partner co-selling looks a lot like traditional value engineering. Meaning, through discovery, you collect a lot of input from the customer about their problem and their business to create a value-based solution. You are not selling widgets; you are selling the solution to your customer's problems.

Our example problem in this chapter is churn, so focus the entire discovery process for this new sales cycle on understanding this customer's churn problem. That way, you can help diagnose the problem and prescribe a solution to a high-value problem. Churn is a good example of the kind of problem you want to solve because it has a demonstrable and measurable financial impact on the bottom line of a company. You must understand and define that impact in order to drive home the value of fixing it.

The other important point to remember is that, if your partner introduced you to the customer and not the other way around, you should be able to source a lot of information ahead of time from the referring partner. This will condense the discovery process and position you as an expert looking to validate proactive research into the situation.

This is vastly different than walking into a meeting as an interrogator, bluntly trying to get the facts and starting with the most basic questions. This can make the customer think, "Didn't you guys talk at all about this before meeting with me?" You want to look good, and you want to make your partner look good. After all, one of you put their customer relationship on the line in order to secure this conversation.

Next, you will want to agree right up front about how you're going to measure success in this introduction. Here are a few ideas:

- Does the customer accept the meeting?
- Do they validate that we have a legitimate solution to their problem?
- Does the sales cycle operate faster than our typical cycle?
- Do we win the deal?
- Does the deal have good margin? (Remember, you might now be compensating a partner for their role.)

"Despite the fact that I was very lucky to learn to build partnerships in a very data-driven way, the majority of partnership folks were not. I first noticed this when I was interviewing more than 100 people for partner manager roles and I saw they could talk the talk. But they seemed to really just be about 'wine and cheese' partnerships – in other words, good at building relationships and taking each other out for drinks and dinner, but not good at tying any kind of outcome to that. Since I have a sales background, and because I was trained by Ryan Merton (one of the best partnerships leaders I've ever met in my life), I've very much always tied an outcome to partnerships."

— Greg Portnoy, cofounder and CEO, EULER

Marketing Partnership Success

If you as partners agree on the above parameters up front, and you hit these markers, SHOUT IT FROM THE ROOFTOPS! And by shouting, we mean propping this critical first case study up in the form of internal communications or newsletters, ongoing partner spotlight meetings, lunch-and-learns with sales teams, press releases . . .

anything and everything! Partner co-selling and the results generated are a treasure trove of high-value content waiting to be unlocked.

Let's talk about a few key subtleties when it comes to these communications. First, begin by focusing on your and your partner's internal sales team communications. Integrating your message and successes into these is what is going to scale your partnership faster, or at all. You need to get the word around.

Nothing happens in a partnership without engagement in the field so, in truth, all of the work you've done to this point is for one thing: to provide you with ammunition to engage the field teams, and then, of course, the market. Build a story on the problem, the solution, and, most importantly, how those field teams are going to leverage you and your solutions to make money!

At LeadMD, we used a single-slide format when presenting to the Marketo Go-to-Market teams. It was a proven framework that contained variable fields in which to enter fundamentals necessary to highlight our joint wins, like the customer's name, the sales cycle length, the total contract value of the deal, and, most impactful, how much the partner AE made on the deal. We led with this, so they would listen to the rest of our story. Even though AEs are most interested in compensation, knowing the rest of the story is how they are going to earn that extra money. See Figure 7.1.

So, once they know they are going to increase their chances of success as well as their compensation as a result of your partnership, AEs will want to be armed with information about how your solution serves the customer, which is the most important part of the presentation. Start with "what's in it for me" so AEs will hear the story that must become part of their repertoire and easily flow off the tongue. When they truly adopt your provided stories within their sales cycles, we get more at-bats with their customers and prospects.

TRICORBRAUN®

Partner Win Wire

Deal Summary

- Marketo Booking: $300,000 x 3 years
- LeadMD Booking: $150,000 Implementation plus $30,000 per month managed service
- Marketo AE: Brandon del Gaudio
- LeadMD AE: Josh Wagner

Deal Dynamics:

- 7-person buying committee (C-suite through analysts)
- 9-month cycle focused on building value of Marketo vs. free Microsoft solution
- Deep dive value analysis across entire cross-functional buying committee.

Value Drivers:

- Increase net new acquisition conversion rates
- Grow share of wallet
- Shorten sales cycle
- Reduce cost per lead
- Realize great marketing efficiency and use of resources
- Drive sales and marketing alignment
- Decrease customer churn
- Projected $12M value creation over 3-year maturity cycle

Figure 7.1 Partner win wire. *Source:* Copyright In Revenue Capital.

> **Pro Tip:** Be an objection handler. In other words, find out what the sales team's top three to five objections are and use them as triggers for the sellers to insert your solution into the conversation as part of the objection-handling process. It's a win-win. Your partner's sellers are positioned as strategic thinkers, not just pitching their own solution, and as a result, you get an introduction to a new prospect.

This is the basic framework for getting the boat in the water with your new partner. Bring a customer to the table, run a great cycle, make the customer successful, tell the story, and get the person who made the referral paid.

Scaling Your Partnership

So, how do you scale this? Every sales team in the world knows prospecting is the key to building a big healthy pipeline.

As the partner ecosystem begins to have legs, your sales team can dramatically multiply their prospecting power by working the contacts that come directly from your partner's sales and customer success teams. Do that, and you create a flywheel that produces warm introductions fueled by one-to-many relationships that scale your prospecting in a way you could never do on your own.

The best partner sales models begin with intentional prospecting into your partner sales and success teams, rather than direct to market. The framework is simple:

- Near term
- Midterm
- Long term

Have a near-, mid-, and long-term plan built with every AE at the partner organization. There are defining characteristics of each of those buckets but, when doing your account planning within them, first and foremost uncover what target accounts fit into which bucket. Then, come up with a clear action plan to jointly address each bucket.

Examples

Near term:

- These are typically accounts in a very active buying cycle, under three months. They have identified their own acute pains, pains that your solution or partner joint value proposition can solve, and have budget allocated to solve those pains.
- The goal here is to get introduced into a sales cycle.

Midterm:

- These are early-stage conversations with an organization that's a fit within your Ideal Customer Profile who has some degree of pain; however, the prospect has not felt pain to the extent that they are actively in a buying cycle. Typically, these accounts are six months to a year out from the potential of a purchase.
- The goal is to initiate partner introductions. They can be effective deal catalysts and accelerators, providing food for thought through outside perspective.

Long term:

- These are organizations who are of course still within your ICP, and are expressing some level of pain or interest, but whose budget cycle or previous commitments place them a year or more out from being able to make purchases. A great example of this looks like an account who currently has an incumbent provider under a longer-term contract but is also expressing dissatisfaction with their solution. The best play here is to provide partners with content, stories, and other valuable assets, some meant for their eyes and some for their customer, which are relevant to these longer-term opportunities. Your objective is to remain top of mind as a would-be solution provider when the time is right.

Note that this is not a binary equation; you are building relationships with these partner employees much like you are with a typical prospect or customer. That's to say, these are people. It's not all business all the time. Dinner, drinks, games, concerts, and events are all fair game when it comes to cracking the code with your partner counterparts. Staying top of mind and accessible is the key; be present, the latest story in the company newsletter is not always enough.

> **Note:** One year at LeadMD, we chartered a bus and took two dozen commercial sales reps to Napa for wine tasting. That trip paid for itself 10 times over in referrals. It's still talked about 10 years later, long after all of us have moved on to other things in our careers.

Operationalizing your new partner is a game of building new relationships. This chapter outlines some things you should do early on to gain some momentum. However, when it comes down to engaging the field, it's a game of consistency and reward. Make friends and help them make money!

Chapter 8

In the Field

Josh Wagner

Although co-marketing is a critical piece of the partner puzzle, real activation and real relationships are forged face-to-face. Joint marketing efforts are tremendous for upleveling the conversation, building your brand identity with a partner, and creating a conversation. If you don't leverage those co-marketing efforts to build actual relationships in the field, you are not getting the most out of them.

Marketo Field Activities

At LeadMD, we put the lion's share of our "sales" efforts into partner field activation. When I say field activation, that's just partner speak for the intentional engagement of customer-facing individuals, the folks who often hold the keys to the customer relationship. It's incredible how many partner programs fail, simply because they underestimate how important these frontline employees are to gaining actual traction with prospects and customers. When is the last time a CEO wholly controlled the customer relationship? Maybe in very early stages or with an incredibly large strategic customer – but beyond those examples, the door to relationships is firmly guarded by the frontline. As such, everything we did began by focusing on building relationships with the sales team at Marketo. Those relationships were the fastest way for us to get access to their customers, who were ultimately our joint ICP customers.

Sellers are a busy and focused group of individuals who do not waste time with things that are not revenue generating. It was my job to help them generate more revenue, but to do so I had to clearly articulate my value to them, over and over and over.

That was the point of field activation. It was to continuously get in front of the sellers at Marketo to demonstrate the value of our services to them first, then to the end customer. My go-to stable of field activities were broken into two buckets:

- Bucket 1: Marketo seller-focused activation
  - Walking the halls: 1× per month
  - Team-based dinners: 1× per quarter
  - Appreciation trips and awards: 1× per year

- Bucket 2: Customer- and prospect-focused activation with Marketo
  - Bespoke customer events: 3–5× per year
  - Road shows: 3–5× per year
  - Traditional large events (i.e. Marketo's Annual Summit): 1× per year

Bucket 1 centers on activities designed to build and enhance relationships with the partner. The goal is to stay top of mind and be their go-to resource for solving the problems of your joint customer. Bucket 2 focuses on working with your partner to activate deeper customer and prospect relationships in the field. The rest of this chapter dives more deeply into these items, one by one.

Walking the Halls

Every month from 2014 to 2019, I spent 3 to 5 days per month at the Marketo offices in San Mateo. Of course, I would prepare for each trip by setting up a few meetings with sellers and leaders within the organization, but the real goal was to walk the halls, meet people, stumble into meetings, and simply raise awareness. Each time I was there, I either deepened a relationship or created a new one. The proximity continually put me top of mind.

> **Note:** No matter how many phone calls, emails, or webinars we'd run, nothing generated pipeline like walking the halls. Being there was an in-your-face reminder of our partnership and showed that I cared enough to invest in face time.

Without fail, multiple people would see me and say, "I was just talking to this prospect about you. We need to talk." While there, I took people to lunch, took walks for coffee, and even did impromptu training for newbies. I never left a trip to San Mateo with fewer than five new opportunities.

Talking with sellers years later who ultimately have become true friends, I learned that they thought that I *was* LeadMD. They knew there was a company behind me delivering the work product, but I had become synonymous with the brand.

I realize that the prevalence of the remote workforce today has resulted in a greatly diminished amount of "in-office" work versus what we capitalized on pre-2021, but nonetheless, taking time to visit folks in person is priceless. Regardless of their location in a big corporate campus or small home office, every minute of physical face time you invest will help build relationships with your partners in a way you simply cannot do over email, phone, or web meeting.

Team-Based Dinners

At least once a quarter, we took a full team or strategic group of sellers from Marketo to a top-flight dinner or a happy hour at a cool location. This was super easy to do in the San Francisco area, as there was no shortage of great food and venues. We'd typically piggyback a dinner on another in-person event so that we could squeeze a little more relationship building out of a trip. Similarly, I would tack these dinners onto my less-formal "walk the halls" trips, as well.

My favorite approach was to invite a specific team out to eat, that team only. If you take a select group of sellers to a nice dinner, the word tends to get around. We would get approached by other team leaders who had heard about the previous night's excursion asking when we'd take their group, or if they could tag along next time. By keeping the invite list controlled, it enabled us to build a buzz of exclusivity for the next visit.

As Marketo matured and began to acquire other companies, there became a sizable group of sellers outside of their San Mateo office headquarters, so we didn't have the same benefit of face time with those groups through our standard California visits. We knew we had to foster the same exposure and get in front of those groups well. Because they were remote, they also presented additional challenges as they didn't have a lot of geographic concentration, so we decided to use a few key industry and company events to re-create that intimacy. The most common were their quarterly business review

(QBR) meetings, large user events like their annual customer summit, or their annual sales kickoff (SKO) meeting. We knew that all sellers were required to be at these company touchpoints.

The QBR was the best in my opinion, because Marketo segmented their macro sales team into smaller geographic teams, aligned to a territory and managed by a dedicated sales director. Every QBR resulted in each geographic team physically assembling together at a city within the team territory. Because it was just their team getting together, there was far less noise surrounding their trip than usually would accompany an annual summit or SKO. QBRs were also not something other partners would typically be aware of and certainly not "sponsor." But because of our insight, we did just that, creating a custom sponsorship that was unique to LeadMD. In exchange for funding a portion their regional get-together, we were granted seats at their team dinner and received access to a portion of their internal meetings during the event. No other partners did this, and it provided us with exclusive access to these sellers and managers while they were in territory planning and strategy mode. This provided an ideal time to get them thinking about how to leverage a partner and work our way into their target account plans.

The dinners at these QBR events were purely focused on building re-lationships. Business talk was not the focus, yet always happened organically. The goal was to create an experience that they'd talk about with the rest of the sales teams. The goodwill we built with the sales organization alone was worth the cost of the dinners we hosted, not to mention the inevitable deal flow that would come out of them.

Appreciation Trips and Awards

Previously in the chapter, we mentioned that it's important to treat your partners as if they are your customers. They require the same level of sales and marketing firepower as your actual customers. Again, the goal is relationship amplification.

Most sellers, especially in Business-to-Business (B2B) Software-as-a-Service (SaaS), are familiar with the concept of annual performance recognition programs such as presidents' club, award trips, and any number of reward tactics used by companies to motivate their sales team beyond their standard compensation. We used the same concept at LeadMD with our partner sales teams. We created sales contests with our partners that ultimately led to award trips and recognition.

Remember previously when we talked about using existing partner sales meetings like QBRs and SKOs to gain access to remote teams? We found that the annual SKO meeting is an amazing way to get access to your entire partner's sales team, all in one place.

We made it a common practice to sponsor the Marketo SKO, but each year we needed to come up with a way to make as big an impact with our sponsorship as possible. This led us to create our own awards, which we would then creatively integrate into their already planned awards program. We wanted to create visibility for those sellers and teams that had included us in the most deals, as well as foster competition among the other reps who would see their peers being recognized.

We did everything from presenting the winners on stage at the SKO with gifts like high-end Scotch or coveted technology like iPads and AirPods to full-on team trips to Lake Tahoe for a weekend of skiing. Trust me, it got people talking and translated to more conversations, better relationships, and more revenue for us because of the partnership.

Those are a few of the key plays we leaned on heavily in the field to activate partners. We also had a couple of go-to event-focused plays that we used successfully with partners to activate customers and stimulate joint pipeline.

Bespoke Customer Events

Think of joint customer events as small, bespoke gatherings with an intentionally curated list of attendees, often peers that share the same job role. The goal of these events was to collaborate with our partner account executives (AEs) in order to invite target prospect accounts in a specific territory to participate in something fun or interesting. The key to making these successful is to ensure the inclusion of one or two very strong customers in order to round out the group. Think creatively here; suites at sporting events, popular shows, cooking classes – they all make for popular draws; when tailored to the preferences of the target invitees, anything is on the table. It really is about using the event to grab the attention of your ideal audience.

For these events, we'd typically target anywhere from 30 to 50 individuals in decision-making or influential roles at any number of target accounts within the geographic proximity of the event. Event planning and location were heavily driven by the territory, number of accounts in the territory, and the types of events in the area. Because we had at least one or two anchor customers committing to attend, the idea was to have the included customers tell our story to the prospects.

Some of our most successful events included private VIP suites at popular baseball games. The pace of baseball lends itself to a very social atmosphere, especially in the catered suites where food and drinks are continually flowing. Some of the ballparks across the United States are unique and have rabid fan bases, which of course helps drive attendance. Securing coveted box seats at a game where tickets are viewed as incredibly difficult or expensive to acquire is beneficial in multiple ways. Of course it helps drive your prospect attendance, but there is also a certain level of quid pro quo individuals feel when you invite them to an elevated experience. Often, they are more open to business conversations at the event, or following it, as they know you went above and beyond to give them something they actually enjoyed.

Having customers there to tell your story helps alleviate awkward pitches or presentations because they are typically very willing to sing your praises while at a cool event to which you've provided their access. It's a win/win, and further amplified by the financial, marketing, and sales firepower that sharing the load with a partner provides.

Road Shows

Road shows can mean a lot of different things. Within the context of activating partners, we have a few ingredients that make up a road show:

- Partner
- Customer
- Location
- Prospects
- Content

The idea behind the road show is leveraging an in-person meeting with a current customer, but then building a series of prospect meetings in the same geographic location in order to piggyback on top of the committed travel time and expenses. Adding a partner to this mix is a great way to further amplify the effectiveness of these activities because it helps concentrate the road show around an ideal joint customer, leverage face time together with that customer to understand the "better together" story, and then leverage that validated story for strategic prospect visits in the area.

I always liked to aim for one customer visit and a minimum of four prospect visits when performing a road show. A residual benefit of the customer visit should be the creation of a solid content asset, which is then co-branded with the partner to communicate the better together narrative and highlight the customer as the hero of the story.

> **Note:** The reason we call this a *road show* is that this is a rinse-and-repeat type of activity that you can easily scale across key locations with your partners multiple times throughout the year. As you build better relationships with your partners in the field, you will identify the partner AEs with the best relationships, who also tend to have the appetite to participate in these types of events.

A little hack that can take a road show to the next level is to leverage your founder as a thought leader, setting them up to deliver educational content rooted in your unique point of view (POV) while on-site with the customer. Depending on the industry, some companies are starved for unique POVs that can actually drive their business forward; because of this the customer may even be willing to host the workshop at their location and allow you to invite other prospects to the event. If possible, you can leverage the customer's story as the foundation of that educational workshop delivered by the founder.

As an example, we have a company within our portfolio that sells to a very blue-collar market. The ideal buyer and decision-maker literally works in a shop and manages massive fleets of vehicles.

This buyer is typically stretched thin, looking for innovation that can affect their shop and their role. They also desperately crave face time within the evaluation and buying processes.

The road show concept works extremely well with this group, and the technology offered by the company in our portfolio resonates best when demonstrated through the lens of an actual customer environment. Every one of their customers uses technology provided by partners within our portfolio company's partner ecosystem. Those customers are actively looking to get more value out of those partner-provided technologies that they have already invested in.

As a result, we have run these road show workshops for the customer on location, involving our founder to provide insights on how to leverage both their technology and the partner technology together to yield exponential results. When the founder is a respected and established expert in the space, as our founder is, it lends a lot of credibility to the content.

Having the founder on the road with both you and the partner also opens the doors for more prospect meetings. It's a play I've seen work incredibly well with the right founder, who is willing to get out into the field with sales to help activate partner relationships.

Traditional Large Events

B2B marketers have heavily relied on events for a long time. As an organization looking to tap into the Cheat Code, it's important that we look at these events through a different lens than traditional B2B marketing. Events – and event marketing – have been worn out and worn down. Attending and exhibiting at conferences and conventions has been the norm for so long that people see it as a best practice, without really measuring the impact it's having.

Even though the pandemic caused a major upheaval in terms of the structure and frequency of events, they've since returned largely to what they were before. The one exception is the birth of hybrid events (leveraging both physical and digital distribution).

In-person events, though, are basically being done the same way they've been done for 50 years. Much of the content is secured in a pay-for-play fashion leading to most content becoming a thinly veiled proxy for advertising, and sponsorships are gobbled up by the big logos and big players that already have a lot of cachet. Typically, if you want to secure speaking at an event, you must be a sponsor and/or have purchased booth space.

So, people get pigeonholed into large booth presences, which are disguised as a turnkey and effective method of marketing. There are set spaces you can choose from, and then limited choices in terms of booth structures or designs. You apply your brand, everyone shows up, and you try to capture as much attendee attention as possible. Thrilling, right? No.

As a seller you become disenfranchised with this entire model because you are looking to build genuine relationships, not scan the badges of attendees who are just there for tchotchkes to bring home to their kids or dog.

The only real way to stand out within that crowd is to do something completely different across the board, but most companies don't go this route because, frankly, they're scared to break the mold. Therein lies your opportunity. To get worthwhile return on investment (ROI) from events, you have to do something that's in line with what your buyer actually enjoys. Wrap the experience you're giving in leisure or fun; even better, do it with a partner.

Join forces with your partners when exhibiting. The power of your data, pipeline, and ideas is only amplified by their data, pipeline, and ideas. This is especially effective if you're a smaller organization and you can piggyback off your partner's size, bank account, and maturity.

There's also no mandate that you need involve only a single partner at an event. We've run events in the past where we've worked with four or five different partners, co-branding and structuring our physical spaces around one another. Think of how dramatically this can increase your brand footprint. Combining forces helps you stand out in terms of the sheer amount of space you'll occupy and the gravity that produces.

When you look at the title or "platinum" sponsors at events, they have the big booth and everyone else gets lost in a sea of sameness. What if you and your partners took four or five 10×10 booths? Suddenly, your group's footprint is larger than that platinum space. You break out of the mold this way, and you create large amounts of visibility for the activations you'll run in those spaces, both of which help you get noticed and get more from the event investment.

Now, from an activation standpoint, how do you get people to come into your booth area? The big secret to success here is to start long before the event ever does. In the past, we've done sizable giveaways, which always get people's attention. In addition, though, you can pepper in your solutions.

So, let's say you give away a vacation to Hawaii for two, and you give away your bundled service within that. If you have a good complementary partner stack involved, you can give custom services designed on those different parts of the solution. In our case, we had involved multiple software vendors from our partner ecosystem and we designed specific products, health checks, and optimizations that were specific to the software they provided. Therefore, if someone were interested in adopting their software offerings, there we were, with relevant and complimentary services that enabled that adoption.

But even if your partner mix is composed of purely software offerings, you can take it a step further and put together a cooperative road map for the "dream technology stack." Gather together the necessary partners and discount all of your solutions when purchased together, or offer a planning workshop, or a budget approval framework, tools that enable customers to better leverage your offerings together. The options are limitless.

The point is, you want to integrate what you do with what is likely to get people more excited, and then devise a way to combine your activation or offering with your partners to offer something unique that no one else can. If you can combine those aspects, you can uproot the monotony that is large events. So many people just don't think outside the box and feel like they have to fall back on tired strategies, but these just don't perform well anymore.

Once you have a creative and valuable strategy together, think through what you'll do to lure people in. You could try something as simple as a bingo card, where the person has to get a stamp from every single partner within your event ecosystem; similarly, we've also done poker runs among partner booths with great results. But make sure to start these types of efforts well ahead of time. Maybe you begin with a custom landing page and then mail the attendees the aspects that they'll need to play your game on-site at the event.

In other words, activation starts far before someone steps foot within that event. You can leverage print, mailers, as well as digital, so really start to think about your approach in a cross-channel yet holistic manner. By partnering, you're also scaling up all these different channels because each participating partner is messaging their database and driving participation. So, what would have been 50 000 invites turns into 250 000 pretty quickly. That's the power of ecosystems.

Final Thoughts

Becoming successful with events requires reframing your idea of what events are all about. They're not about getting leads; they're about building relationships. Your job isn't to close a deal or provide demos of your solution. Your job is to get your target buyers to remember you when you follow up to set a meeting, or whatever your next action happens to be. Start thinking in terms of amplifying your presence, message, and relationship on-site to drive results long after the event ends.

How do you get in there and share those relationships with all the partners who are participating? And then, how do you ultimately leverage those relationships to open the doors to a joint solution that's truly going to help that organization and that buyer?

Remember that relationships are gold. Truly understanding a business comes as a result of getting to the bottom of the customer's fundamental needs, desires, and goals. What do they want to be as an organization? What are they trying to do? What are their strategic initiatives?

Most sellers might be able to answer that through a very myopic lens, but only in terms of the things that matter to them; they often don't go wide enough to truly understand the organization and the people who operate within it. The only way to do that is to share that work-load among partners that serve the same buying committee, the same buyer, the same strategic goals of the customer.

It doesn't matter if you deploy all or some of these plays to activate partners in the field; the point of this entire chapter is that in order for partnerships to be successful, it takes real, tactical, face-to-face effort, focused on building real relationships. The activation of those relationships is then imperative for a partnership to truly bear fruit.

Chapter 9

The Relationship Recipe

Justin Gray

There's one fundamental aspect of partnerships that should seem inherent by this point, but shouldn't ever be glossed over. Of course I'm speaking about the relationship element underneath the business transactions. We've talked quite a bit about the power of relationships in this book, and it might sound painfully obvious, but the reality is that many folks make assumptions about what a relationship truly is, or how they are formed, that are often just plain wrong.

First, in business I find that many professionals assume that simply being on friendly terms with someone means you have a relationship. Maybe you regularly exchange comments about a shared related interest (e.g. sports) in your emails, or you "like" and comment on one another's LinkedIn posts. This might be a doorway into getting to know someone, but it's all superficial. These are not the makings of real relationships, at least not the kind you need for winning partnerships.

Second, many people today assume that digital connection is just as valid as in-person connection. This feeling was only perpetuated by the global pandemic, as society was collectively forced to take face-to-face interactions, both personal and professional, and conduct them digitally.

We're not here to lambast digital tools. They're enormously important and, if you can't meet in person, there are plenty of times when using Zoom or FaceTime or Slack can be the most efficient route – and still somewhat effective. But when it comes to forming and maintaining relationships that you hope to turn into partnerships? There is no substitute for time together in person.

This chapter discusses what it really takes to create the solid relational foundations on which your partnerships can be built.

The Value of Proximity

When you hear that you need to prioritize in-person togetherness, you might balk. It doesn't sound practical. After all, perhaps you're based in North Carolina and most of the potential partners you have your eye on are in San Francisco.

Or maybe your own team is entirely remote, spread across the United States, and so are the companies with whom you'd love to partner. Proximity can sound great in theory, but there's only so much you can do given geographical barriers . . . right?

Well, it's true that this is the mindset that most people have. But those who want to have strong partnerships and wield the Cheat Code successfully aren't most people. In fact, you have to be willing to do the things that others won't if you want to get the outcomes that others don't have. Let's dig into what this looks like in practice.

One example would be moving your company's entire Go-to-Market (GTM) function to the Bay Area because that's where your ideal partners are located. I know this works, because I did it at LeadMD for a period of four years. The only way you truly understand what they're dealing with daily, below the surface of passing conversations and quarterly updates, is by being on-site with these individuals. Once you do that, you can harvest their pain points and construct your value propositions specifically tailored to what will solve them and help your partner perform better in their role (and perform better as a company).

Another example is gathering your own team and going to a given area to carve out quality time with a potential partner that you wouldn't naturally have otherwise. Maybe your team is remote but a prospective partner's team is largely based on the other side of the country. It's your job to get everyone together.

Even if there's no physical office, make the trip and rent out a restaurant or a coworking space that's convenient for them and invite all the reps in for the day to work and spend time together. You'll probably find that there are natural geographical clusters that arise when you analyze your partner's team distributions, and therefore you can devise a plan to hit those in order of highest priority.

Remember, too, that this doesn't just apply to events. As a matter of fact, it shouldn't be event-centric at all. Everyone sets meetings when at conferences and trade shows, and this can be valuable (see Chapter 8), but this is different.

This is about getting face time with strategic partners proactively and on your own dime and time. It's much harder to compete for attention at events, and interactions are diluted in such formats anyway. You need to take the initiative to create your own forum. Again, do what other people aren't doing.

The Relationship Recipe

It's worth noting, also, that many people are getting back into offices. Yes, hybrid and remote work environments are still a thing, but there are a lot of companies encouraging, if not mandating, that their team members spend the majority of their work days in a physical office again. If this is the case for a partner, you need to be there, too.

Back in the early days of LeadMD, we were in the Marketo offices so much that people thought we were part of the Marketo team. We didn't move our entire lives to their headquarters, but we did plan regular trips when we would spend whole days in their office building, working from there, sitting in on meetings and absorbing everything we possibly could about what matters to them on a day-to-day basis.

Even if you get the gist of this idea, it might sound weird, like you have to invite yourself to camp out at someone else's company. That's okay. Most likely, you are going to have to take the initiative because most people don't ask for this level of proximity. But again, that's not a bad thing. You're not trying to be like most people. You're trying to get to know your potential partners in a very in-depth and uncommon way.

Explain to the prospective partner that you want to learn as much as you can about them, their role, and their organization so you can determine how to bring maximum value to your working relationship. Ask them for something specific, like a desk where you can set up for four work days a month. You'll be surprised by the willingness – and even the delight – this can yield, in addition to the stage it will set for the rich future of your partnership.

The Relational Mindset

You can try all these tactics, but these relationships won't work without humility. There are so many founders who take the myopic view that "*my* world is *the* world," and they expect partners to shapeshift into a mold of their choosing. This approach will never work and will actually damage relationships rather than kickstart them.

From the beginning of my entrepreneurial journey, I've adopted the exact opposite mindset. I've seen myself as the outsider, because I often am. Every business I've started has been my first foray into that industry, vertical, or business model. Thus, I look at the company that has a lot of gravity in the space, that has access to my buyer, and that I want to get close to, and ask myself, how can I get into their circle of trust? This manifests in really simple ways.

Rewarding partnerships start with the mentalities we have and the relationships that spring from them. For instance, I was reviewing deals with a rep the other day and asked why they didn't engage the partner. The buyer had gone dark, and without a partner attached we had no place to turn for additional insights. I couldn't understand why there wasn't intuitive partner involvement, but honestly, it's just not a natural inclination for most reps. They're not trained to think in that manner, and they need to be inspired and almost indoctrinated to believe that they'll be "better together."

Once you and your reps are thinking in terms of partnership first, you'll start to rewire your efforts on inclusion rather than exclusion. You begin asking how you'll get exposure to the right people. As an example, we largely didn't hire people in Arizona when we made hires at LeadMD, even though the founding team was based there. This is because we wanted people on the ground where the early adopters of Marketo were located, because we knew being close to them was going to matter in very important ways.

Additionally, you have to be aware of the life cycles an organization is going through, which is something else you can ascertain much more easily when you're on-site. What is going on within the walls of a strategic partner? Are they trying to shift the culture in a certain way?

In the early days of LeadMD, Marketo was trying to get more of that marketing DNA in the organization rather than just technologist DNA – so that knowledge in turn affected the folks that we hired. We had to make sure they fundamentally understood the minds and priorities of chief marketing officers in order to augment our strategic partner with the skills they lacked. We had to ensure they were well versed in marketing strategy and had been in board meetings before.

If you can build your teams to fulfill the skills needed to accomplish the goals your partners have, the more natural the relationship will become. This enables your organization to become the purpose-built resource your partner needs. Quite frankly, these are aspects you don't get insight into unless you're sitting in the middle of someone's office as they're having calls and discussing the problems they're facing.

You have to find ways to mine that. Everyone says, "customer first" and preaches about getting in the mindset of the customer. But you'll move so much slower toward that goal if you're not also talking to the people who already have access to the headspace of those customers.

Show Them They Matter

Once you've built the basis of a relationship by spending time together and investing your energy into what your strategic partner cares about, you must reinforce your value proposition through every possible avenue. Consider how you can stay visually top of mind and raise the stories that will resonate with the partner's needs.

In the past, my team and I have used benchmarking and data science to hone in on partner key performance indicators (KPIs), demonstrating how we could improve them together. I've found that many of our partners had strategic business goals based on the improvement of metrics they actually didn't have or didn't understand. We took it on ourselves to plug those gaps and then proactively improve performance in those areas. Think about this at various levels: role-based and department-based, in particular.

How can you influence KPIs at each? And how do you embed this sort of dashboard within the partner's vision? In other words, you're essentially building your business in order to optimize the metrics of a true strategic partner. If you do this, it will make it incredibly difficult to ignore you.

Throughout our work in partnerships, it's also become clear that innovators don't skate to where the puck is; they go where others aren't. For instance, sales kickoffs unlocked entire relationships for us. As Josh described in Chapter 8, no one was sponsoring them back then, so we did – and then went beyond mere sponsorship to also create our own sales contest for participants. He also talked about the creation of the sales contests for our strategic partners. But beyond the immediate impact these tactics had, the fact that our leaderboards and dashboards were embedded everywhere their own sales metrics were displayed enabled us to truly erase the line between us and them.

We made partners, specifically our partnership, synonymous with standard sales practice. Because we had created the understanding that when Marketo software was sold, the best way to ensure the customer's success was to attach a partner who would manage the implementation process, we knew a services partner was going to be attached. By ensuring that "referrals to LeadMD" was a KPI that appeared everywhere performance was tracked and then coupling that performance with outsized rewards in the form of trips and trinkets, we stacked the deck in our favor.

> **Tip:** What does this all boil down to? It's simple, really. It's about rewarding partners in ways that truly make them feel valuable. When you do this, you knit together relationships that stick throughout careers. When a partner goes on to form other companies, the relationships stay intact, because they're so meaningful.

Still, you have to remember there's no magic bullet. You can't just send someone a trunk full of swag and expect to forge a lasting connection. You need to be consistent in your approach and in the value you provide while seizing every opportunity to be near them and provide value. This is the investment you'll continue to make over the life of the partnership.

That's what partnership is, after all. Partners hold the key to your buyer and your revenue, and vice versa. When those relationship bonds are strong, you're selling and servicing more deals. When it's weak, your revenue line is being threatened.

But when you're building these relationships, prospective partners will be able to easily discern if your approach is driven by lust or true love. Offer value and make their job easier, consistently. After all, you can do things that they can't do in-house and yet the customer wants those things, so be generous with that value. Don't wait to get something from them first. Investing proactively, or "giving to get," is the most effective marketing dollar that you'll ever spend. Because if you lock down one truly strategic relationship, that opens the doors to deals, introductions, and further relationships for years to come, if all goes well.

Add Value Above All

Don't just pop up every time you need something. Throughout my career, my teams and I have regularly delivered real tangible value to partners even when there would be no return in kind, just to help them out and to build stronger relationships. We did this all the time with our value engineering offering.

Many of our strategic partners had to put together a true business case, a bulletproof return-on-investment model used to convince a prospect of the value their solution would yield. These models were much more complex than just stating the costs of technology and the costs associated to implement it. These cost of ownership and forecasted results models had to hold up in the board room. We would help them build this, clearly illustrating how the technology would integrate with everything else that they were doing, along with how it amplified their core GTM strategies and the ultimate returns it would generate. We would generate an extremely comprehensive analysis that would stand up to scrutiny from a board of directors or chief financial officer who knows the profit and loss statement like the back of their hand.

This would be impossible to ask a young technology salesperson to do. We truly were their outsourced value engineering team, but we did a lot of this pro bono, on deals that were almost certainly not going to come to us. We did it because our strategic partner was struggling and they were likely to lose the deal if we didn't augment their gaps.

This is the gold standard for partnerships. You care about the partner as much as you care about your own success, and you back that up with real action and investment. Adopting the better together mindset is the best place to start, but then you need to be proximal to what matters and go deep into solving for that partner's needs and wants.

Be the one who fills their gaps. Form individual connections that outlast a single stop on their career journey. These are the partnerships, and friendships, that will serve others, serve you, and make a difference.

Chapter 10

When It All Goes Wrong

Josh Wagner

There are good relationships and bad relationships. Partnerships in Business-to-Business (B2B) are no different. When it all goes right, it feels like you have unlocked the ultimate Cheat Code for Go-to-Market (GTM) growth and efficiency. When it all goes wrong . . .

We've all been in a bad relationship. It doesn't start badly, or at least you didn't think it did, but when you sit back and reflect, you realize all the signs were there. You just couldn't see them. Like any relationship, we go into them with the best of intentions, but they don't always work.

Justin and I have worked through all of the key components in a successful B2B partnership, so you can naturally draw a line to where they might fall down. I can tell you 9 times out of 10 the culprit is culture (Chapter 5), lack of top-down buy-in (Chapter 3), or a combination of the two.

The top-down necessity that Justin outlines in Chapter 3 really does set the table for successful partner culture in a company. If you are honest with yourself, you can probably feel it's going wrong before anything really ugly shows up. But if you don't get ahead of what your instincts are telling you, there could be a big blow up on the horizon, one detrimental to your GTM success.

Signs It's Going Wrong

Before we get into a disaster story, let's first take a look at some of the telltale signs that things are just not headed in the right direction with a partner. The most common sign is that the "partnership" seems very one-sided; you are giving a lot, but there seems to be no interest in reciprocation.

You can usually identify this very early in a partnership, if you use my favorite partner qualifier from the jump. That is, we don't start a partnership until we test our joint solution with a customer. My company brings a customer to the table; your company brings a customer to the table. It's that simple and a very effective way to sniff out how the organization and the people within it think about partnership.

There is a method to this madness. Doing this has yielded the best results by far and on every occasion, without fail. When I have failed to stick to my guns on this with a potential partner, the partnership goes nowhere. The reason it's so important is simple. It's the key to unlocking the important ingredient we discussed in Chapter 4, right from the beginning.

If you recall, executive buy-in is the first ingredient in the setup of your Cheat Code. If the executive team is not bought into partnerships at all levels, the idea of bringing one of their customers to the table to validate the partnership will be a no go. The bigger the organization, the more rigidity in the partner program, the bigger the pushback you are going to get on this seemingly simple ask.

Executive teams not bought into a holistic, organization-wide approach to partnerships view partners almost exclusively a lead source; that's about it. Leveraging one of their customers to test the value of a new partner is counterintuitive in their mind because the value of a partner is to bring them business, not involve business they've already won.

Lack of executive buy-in will rear its ugly head early, and if you are aware and honest with yourself, you can react to it before you expend too much time and effort on a partnership going nowhere. This is a cultural barrier that is really tough to overcome. Nonetheless, let's review the second ingredient in the setup of your Cheat Code: the Ideal Partner Profile (IPP) exercise.

The primary driver in that exercise is proximity to your Ideal Customer Profile (ICP). The customer exchange play is an easy way to share the data points of your ICP with a customer you are willing to bring to the table that matches this ICP. If they are unable to surface the same type of ICP accounts then there might be an issue.

The third ingredient (the give-to-get mentality) is a no-brainer here. If you are willing to give up a customer to test your joint solution, then they should be willing to do the same. Maybe you are the much smaller player going to play with the big boys, in which case you can offer a 2:1 exchange. But this is another proof point on executive buy-in and cultural fit with your potential partner.

> **Tip:** There is a big red flag to look out for here that might mask itself as "give to get." The partner manager on the other side offers to "share lists" instead of sharing a specific customer. The act of list sharing is the biggest farce in the partner ecosystem. It's a way to pacify the partner by offering up a list of customers and prospects so you can look for crossover. I have never seen anything meaningful come from this exercise. Frankly, when you are establishing

a new partnership, the value is the proximity to a customer in a hands-on, white glove manner. Scouring a list of company names to see which might fit your ICP – and who they might have a good relationship with – is not how partners act. Period.

The real purpose of this customer exchange is to activate ingredients four and five of your Cheat Code setup. Joint Value Proposition (JVP) creation is highly dependent on customer feedback. We can make all the assumptions in the world about the gaps our solutions can fill and our "better together" message, but if there is no real, tangible feedback and validation of that message, there is a good chance it falls flat. By bringing respective customers to the table, we are running an experiment against what we believe to be true about this partnership.

Note: I should point out the importance of customer selection and expectation setting as a part of this experiment. This should never be an at-risk customer; actually, it should be the opposite. Look for a best-fit, super-happy customer, one who leans on you for insights and solutions and is open to experimentation.

This handoff process is bound to be bumpy, so let them know upfront. We will be testing our JVP, so let them know. We will be testing our co-sell process, so let them know. These are critical conversations you must have with your customer. Similarly, our partner should be doing the same. This is the best way to test, iterate, and validate the partner thesis.

Finally, the rubber meets the road at field activation. If this works well, the output of this exercise should be two success stories – stories that you will package up in a variety of formats to take the new partnership to market. You now have something tangible for your marketing team to announce this partnership and build campaigns around. You have a story to tell.

In the same vein, sales is typically reluctant to work with partners, especially if there is nothing more than an idea present. However, a fully baked and validated "better together" story that demonstrates how they win, win more, and make more money is a great way to engage the field, as we outlined in prior chapters.

It might seem simple that each partner must bring a customer to the table. But it's just as simple to look past it. By doing so, you are fast-forwarding through critical visibility of all the potential pitfalls of the partnership. Each ingredient outlined is a window into how and if the partnership will work. It's a qualifier – it's a chance to save time, money, and countless cycles with a non-fit partner.

A Cautionary Tale of Partner Program Misalignment

I was personally on the wrong end of this in 2017 with a certain large Software-as-a-Service Customer relationship management (CRM) provider. I won't mention the name specifically here but they're the largest in the world. (Okay, fine, you guessed it – it was Salesforce.) LeadMD had been a part of their partner program for several years. That simply meant that we had the privilege of sending them deals and earning a referral commission for doing so. As a services company whose offerings were designed to support all of the major marketing and sales technologies, this was a very common occurrence among large software providers: a "referral program" masked as a partner program.

We didn't have the size or scale to be considered as a part of their solution partner network, which in theory had greater benefits. We were relegated to lead registration. When we registered a lead we'd then get a call or email from the assigned sales rep asking for an information download on the prospect. We'd provide it, and they'd take it from there. There was rarely much of a partner co-sell cycle because the account executives (AEs) were trained to take the lead and close it as fast as possible. It really didn't matter to them that we held the customer relationship.

Occasionally, we'd get a call from the seller asking when the referred prospect was going to sign their contract. They hadn't included us in the deal to that point, but now that they hadn't closed on their preferred timeline, all of a sudden, we were being asked to be their magic bullet. Not exactly a "give-to-get" relationship.

In 2013, Salesforce had acquired a competitor to Marketo called Pardot, which had previously been acquired by ExactTarget. As a way to stimulate growth, Salesforce sellers were highly incentivized to sell the new Pardot solution into their existing customer base along with heavily incentivizing new customers to add it in addition to their CRM subscription.

Jumping forward again to 2017, I had an existing customer who was looking for help with the deployment of marketing automation. We had helped them evaluate options and ultimately selected Marketo as their best option, but we also suggested they make a move to Salesforce CRM at the same time in order to get the most out of their investment. During this cycle, I had worked very closely with the AE at Marketo to design the solution based on the specifications necessary to drive growth within their organization. By this time we had hardened all other elements of their technology stack, and the only missing piece was Salesforce CRM.

Given my prior experiences working with Salesforce AEs, I didn't want to engage them early (huge red flag, I know) because all they cared about was winning the contract, not co-designing a solution. At this point, Salesforce was the clear market leader. Their outlook on the market was dominant; it wasn't a question of *if* a company was going to buy Salesforce, but *when*. Sellers took that to heart, and they were not interested in a referral conversation unless it was clearly going to close in a short amount of time.

So, I followed their process, registered the lead, and was assigned to the seller who owned the territory, a person I didn't have any type of relationship with in any way. They reached out to schedule a call. I set the call and packaged everything up for them in a way that clearly demonstrated to them that we knew the customer, had designed the solution, and even shared our implementation plan. It was just a matter of getting a proposal for the specified software package we had recommended. It was a slam dunk, a ready to close deal for the partner, a scenario you would think would be their dream.

We did make one ask, which was "please don't try to sell Pardot to this customer." We were clear; we designed this solution with Salesforce and Marketo as the key pillars in the technology plan for their digital transformation initiative. Everything I had built previously with the Marketo AE was designed to provide a win for us, them, and Salesforce, before the end of the quarter.

We gave the Salesforce team ample time to perform their own customer discovery and validation of our proposed solution. We had plenty of runway to allow for the execution of agreements within the timeline we'd built. Therefore, once we made the hand-off of the customer to the Salesforce AE, we left it to them to run their part of the cycle. In fact, the customer requested that we hand them off at that point, saying we did not need to waste our time in the CRM buying process.

BIG MISTAKE. We'd set time with the customer to debrief after their calls with Salesforce to ensure there were no issues with the CRM proposal, timeline, or scope of work. I guess Salesforce underestimated the relationship we had with the customer. Not only did they recommend Pardot to the customer, but they recommended the customer work with another "more qualified" implementation partner. They tried to kick us out of our own deal!

Although they were unsuccessful due to the strength of our relationship with the customer, it did derail our original timeline for the deal. Salesforce hadn't acted in partnership; instead, they were stubborn and greedy, going so far as to say that they could not sell them CRM without Pardot or a qualified partner attached to the deal. Justin and I had to waste time and energy not just fighting this with the AE, but also with his manager who was supportive of this behavior.

Unfortunately, we missed closing the deal by the end of the quarter because of this fiasco, which made a huge dent in my quota achievement for the quarter; the same was true for the AE at Marketo, who was counting on the deal to hit his goals. Unlike his Salesforce counterpart, the involved Marketo AE was a person I trusted and respected and who had behaved as a true partner the entire way.

This is an extreme example, but literally none of the Cheat Code setup ingredients were in place here. We were a cog in the wheel, a low-level partner in a vast referral program at Salesforce, which meant we were nothing more than a lead source to them. In fact, if we provided them a lead, it was theirs to do with as they pleased, in their minds. There was ZERO chance we were ever getting anything in return that even remotely resembled a relationship from that "partnership."

Unfortunately, given the proximity and technical dependencies Marketo had with Salesforce, we had to support the platform. We also got a fair amount of work from customers who were unhappy with the "more qualified" services partner the Salesforce AE had suggested, only to be let down by them. We often had to unwind their mess, costing the customer more time and money to fulfill the promise of CRM.

Let this be a cautionary tale. The Cheat Code is only a cheat if there are true relationships in place. The customer exchange early in the partner vetting process is designed explicitly to help drive alignment and forge those solid relationships.

Chapter 11

Success and the New Metrics

Justin Gray

If relationships are the currency of success, what are the agreed-on precursors of a strong relationship? Moreover, how do you truly measure that success? Let's go a little broader to start. Sales, marketing, partnerships, and businesses are built on trust.

Trust Is the Foundation

In fact, trust is the foundation on which every strategy outlined in this book relies. In today's world, where data is considered the new oil, trust has become the new data. Without trust, none of the approaches and tactics mentioned in this book are possible.

However, trust is a complex concept that is difficult to define and quantify. There are no clear, measurable metrics that can accurately capture the essence of trust. Nevertheless, this chapter aims to shed light on the concepts and practices that have consistently proven to foster trust and accelerate partnerships, as well as to assign reliable markers for the measure of something that's often framed as intangible.

There are three precursors for the establishment of trust that we explore in this chapter:

- A "pipeline for life" mindset
- Outward focus
- Emotional intelligence

Figure 11.1 shows these three markers.

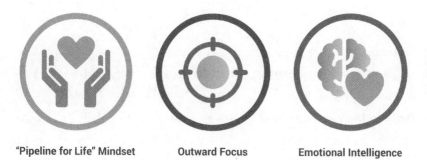

"Pipeline for Life" Mindset   Outward Focus   Emotional Intelligence

Figure 11.1   The three primary markers of trust. *Source:* Copyright In Review Capital.

A Pipeline for Life Mindset

The concept of the pipeline for life mindset is based on playing the long game. Too often, businesses become fixated on short-term gains, focusing only on the immediate month, quarter, or year. In doing so, they overlook the immense value of building meaningful relationships.

Alternately, establishing and nurturing relationships is the cornerstone of the pipeline for life mindset. Every interaction, however small, holds intrinsic value, even if it might not yield immediate results. For instance, during my tenure at LeadMD, because we had become known as the Go-to Marketing (GTM) and revenue operations consultancy in the space, I would receive an enormous amount of inbound interest from GTM professionals seeking advice, seeking insight on topics ranging from what was working in Business-to-Business, all the way down to how to get their next job. These inquiries ranged from students to executives at enterprise organizations. Because of the brand we had built, I had the opportunity to engage with approximately a dozen new individuals each week. Many of them might not have had any intention to buy marketing services from us in the near future, and some were not a fit to become customers at all. Still, I recognized the long-term value in every interaction – the potential relationship and the value it might one day yield.

Relationships have a compounding effect; each person you connect with opens up access to their own network. A robust and well-connected network is valuable, not solely because of the number of people it comprises, but due to its potential to facilitate mutually beneficial connections between individuals. In other words, your network's true value lies in the ability to help others by leveraging the diverse expertise and resources of the people within it.

In the real world, this mindset translates into recognizing the significance of happy customers. Not only do they provide immediate value through additional purchases and licenses as they succeed and grow but they also create an exponential ripple effect within their own networks.

Furthermore, relationships are constantly evolving due to employee attrition, acquisitions, and liquidity events. As talent naturally migrates and shifts between organizations, these connections continue to nourish and enrich your pipeline for life.

Outward Focus

Another crucial aspect of building trust is maintaining an outward focus. This involves prioritizing the needs and concerns of others over personal interests. It's about genuinely seeking to understand and address the challenges and goals of your partners, customers, and peers. By demonstrating empathy and actively listening, you create an environment of trust and collaboration.

When you shift your focus to the needs of others, it not only strengthens the bonds within your relationships but also enhances your own problem-solving capabilities. By understanding the pain points and aspirations of your partners, you can identify opportunities for mutual growth and develop innovative solutions to address their specific challenges.

Emotional Intelligence

Just like in other interpersonal relationships outside of work, emotional intelligence plays a vital role in establishing and nurturing trust in business. It encompasses self-awareness, empathy, and the ability to regulate and manage emotions effectively. By cultivating emotional intelligence, you can develop a deep understanding of your partners' needs, motivations, and concerns. This understanding enables you to tailor your approach and communication style to build stronger connections and foster trust.

Emotional intelligence also enables you to navigate challenging situations with grace and diplomacy. It helps you manage conflicts constructively, seek mutually beneficial outcomes, and respond empathetically to feedback. By demonstrating emotional intelligence, you create an environment that fosters trust, open communication, and collaboration within your partnerships.

In conclusion, trust is the cornerstone of successful sales, marketing, partnerships and overall business growth. Embracing the mindset of the pipeline for life, prioritizing outward focus, and developing emotional intelligence can all contribute to building and nurturing trust. By doing so, you lay the foundation for long-term, mutually beneficial relationships that drive sustainable success in the ever-evolving business landscape.

Tip: Remember, trust is not easily defined by quantitative metrics but is rather a holistic and multifaceted concept that transcends traditional measurements.

As investors, we recognize the presence of – or untapped potential in – partner ecosystems as a critical lever in our investment rubric. Why? Because we firmly believe that for founders, partnering is the fastest way to achieve scalable growth. Although traditional outbound strategies and the effectiveness of inbound marketing might fluctuate, the value of relationships remains constant.

As highlighted in Chapter 10, partnerships are built on relationships and relationships are built on trust. By leveraging the power of partnerships, we can create an exponential growth lever in our own businesses and those of our partners, achieving results that surpass the simple sum of 1 plus 1.

Measuring the Success of Partnerships

With this understanding in mind, the question remains: how can we determine if a partnership is truly successful? How do we measure success within this new world of collaborative ecosystems?

Measuring the success of a partnership can be challenging, especially in the early stages. However, by understanding the finish line, we can properly establish the mentality necessary to start and win the race. As such, the wise old saying "what gets measured gets managed" serves as a valuable reminder that in order to see the impact of these *new* metrics of trust tomorrow, we also have to ensure we have a benchmark of how they perform today. To overcome this hurdle, let's work backward from the ultimate goal and identify the key metrics that will be critical in gauging success within our partner ecosystem.

Two core business metrics hold significant importance in this context:

- Customer Acquisition Cost (CAC)
- Customer Lifetime Value (CLV)

Customer Acquisition Cost

CAC is the amount of money a company invests to acquire a new customer. It quantifies the Return on investment (ROI) generated from efforts to expand the customer base. Calculating CAC involves adding up the costs associated with converting prospects into customers, such as marketing, advertising, sales personnel, and more. This total cost is then divided by the number of customers acquired during a given period.

Establishing a robust partner ecosystem can have an extreme impact on reducing CAC. However, to gauge the effectiveness of your partnership endeavors in this regard, it is essential to have a benchmark CAC.

Tip: To calculate your CAC, you can use a simple formula: add the costs of sales and marketing, all of the costs, and then divide that sum by the number of customers acquired over the same period of time. This will provide you with a baseline from which you can assess the impact of your partner ecosystem on lowering CAC.

Customer Lifetime Value

CLV is the predicted net profit that a company can expect to generate over the course of its relationship with a customer. It helps determine the long-term value of acquiring and retaining customers. Calculating CLV involves analyzing various factors, such as average purchase value, purchase frequency, customer lifespan, and gross margin. By understanding the CLV of your customers, you can draw insights into the revenue potential they bring to your business.

A flourishing partner ecosystem can significantly contribute to increasing CLV by driving customer loyalty and engagement. The collaborative efforts and resources shared within the partnership can enhance the overall customer experience and increase the value customers derive from your products or services. By continuously nurturing and deepening these relationships, you create a foundation for long-term customer retention and loyalty.

We hope you can see that partner ecosystems are game changers in today's business landscape. By strategically building and nurturing partnerships based on trust, you can unlock immense growth potential. Evaluating the success of your partner ecosystem requires a focus on key business metrics, such as CAC and CLV.

Analyzing these metrics in the context of your partnership initiatives will provide valuable insights into the impact of your collaborative efforts on scalability and profitability. Remember, partner ecosystems are not merely a means to an end but rather a catalyst for continuous growth and innovation in the ever-evolving business landscape.

As outlined in this book, the effectiveness of traditional inbound and outbound efforts is diminishing over time, leading to an increase in CAC for Software-as-a-Service companies. This means that the payback period to acquire a customer is getting longer, decreasing the impact of their Annual recurring revenue (ARR).

In response to these changes, investors are now seeking capital-efficient founders who can demonstrate the ability to grow while preserving capital and extending runway as much as possible. Contracting CAC has become a crucial lever in achieving this goal.

Once you have established your CAC benchmark, it's important to start tracking partner attachment rates, influenced and sourced opportunities, deal velocity, and customer acquisition by partner. This enables you to develop a less mature but valuable metric for tracking partner success – the number of partner-involved logos and revenue.

Meanwhile, it's equally important to ensure you are tracking the full costs associated with nurturing and managing your partnerships, enabling you to establish the complete picture for calculating ROI in terms of CAC. By applying the same simple CAC formula and evaluating that by each partner, as well as in aggregate, as you do to your other Go-to-Market (GTM) channels, you can determine if CAC by partner is performing significantly lower, indicating the effectiveness of your partnership strategy.

Let me predict the future for you briefly. Partner channel CAC will be lower, often substantially by a factor of half or more. Absolutes are always tricky, and often a recipe for foolishness, but I have never seen a successful partner ecosystem where CAC does not outperform all other channels. Why? The reason ecosystems are so effective goes back to our core partnership premise. Outbound is interruptive and hence extremely inefficient; inbound is designed to attract and therefore difficult to perfect and maintain, leading to equal inefficiency. Both of these strategies are extremely expensive due to the fact that you first have to get the prospect's attention and then they require the buyer to change their behavior. Partner ecosystems, however, surround the buyer through access granted by trusted relationships. You meet the buyer where they are so it's not a stretch to understand why my confidence is so high in terms of partner efficiency.

Now let's shift our focus to CLV as the other crucial metric in assessing partnership success. Why CLV? Because although CAC measures net new revenues driven by partners, CLV provides a more holistic approach by considering the overall value of partner-enabled customer acquisition and management. In essence, CLV is the inverse of CAC as we strive for increased CLV in terms of duration and monetary value.

Expanding the CLV of customers is where the true benefits of partnerships come into play. By fostering strong relationships and collaborative efforts with partners, you not only increase customer loyalty and retention but also enhance the overall customer experience. This can lead to increased purchase frequency, higher Average contract values (ACV), reduced churn, and, ultimately, a boost in customer CLV. Partnerships create an ecosystem that envelops customers, offering them added value, support, and a sense of community – factors that drive long-term engagement and higher CLV.

In conclusion, CAC and CLV are two critical metrics that materialize the success equation when it comes to partnerships. By diligently tracking and analyzing CAC, both with and without partner involvement, you can assess the impact of your partnership strategy on lowering spend. Simultaneously, focusing on increasing CLV through partnerships ensures a comprehensive approach to measuring success based on growth. Together they manifest fundamental business metrics that make sense both in and outside of the boardroom.

When you guide your partner focus by these markers, strategically nurturing the partnerships that perform, you maximize customer loyalty and engagement, leading to extended customer life cycles and increased revenue potential. Remember, partnerships offer not only revenue benefits but also an enriched customer experience that has the potential to drive exponential growth and long-term success.

CLV is a vital business metric that quantifies the anticipated earnings a company can derive from an average customer over the duration of their relationship. Although the calculations for CLV can be complex, a simple formula involves multiplying the average customer value by the average customer lifespan. Establishing these benchmarks, particularly in the early stages of your business, makes it easier to compare results from your partner ecosystem.

But why is CLV an essential metric for measuring the success of a partner ecosystem? The answer lies in its ability to account for the difficult dots to connect and therefore often intangible benefits of partnerships. When collaborating with other companies, you're likely to encounter partner teams measuring only *sourced* or *influenced revenue* in an attempt to capture partner success in a very superficial and linear manner.

Yet, this provides a limited perspective on success, and one that kills many partnerships before they can mature. CLV, however, is a comprehensive business metric that enables you to compare the lifespan and value of customers who engage with/through your partners versus those who do not.

CAC and CLV serve as the most mature and effective means to measure the success of partnerships. As you build your partner-enabled business, you'll need to initially look at early indicators such as those *sourced* and *influenced* revenue metrics mentioned previously. The best true leading indicator of long-term success, however, resides in partner attachment rate, the ability to involve one or more partners in every sales cycle and existing customer account. This blanket edict will establish the best chances of not only driving real impact on CAC and CLV but also visibility, volume of opportunities, as well as deal velocity.

Although leading metrics are valuable, they are anything but complete or predictive, particularly if you rely solely on *sourced* revenues as is the industry standard. Such an approach limits the partnership's potential because sourced revenue tends to fluctuate and promotes a myopic view of success. By contrast, CAC and CLV provide a holistic and sustainable lens through which to evaluate true success.

We highly recommend that you encourage the partners within your ecosystem to adopt these same leading as well as lagging measures of success. By aligning on the importance of calibrating short-term indicators against longer-term measures like CAC and CLV, you ensure a shared understanding and approach to assessing the partnership's value. This alignment facilitates a broader perspective on success, maintaining a long-term focus that extends beyond transient fluctuations in engagement and demand. Ultimately, measuring success through CAC and CLV enables both you and your partners to evaluate the true impact of the partnership, and the overall business.

Chapter 12

When It All Goes Right

Josh Wagner

I often hear founders say, "I gave partnerships a try and it didn't work out." But when you dive deeper into the efforts invested into those partnerships, it's often revealed that *try* they did not. All too often the parties signed a referral agreement, maybe built an integration, or possibly tried their hand at some lightweight marketing, perhaps a joint webinar.

As we've tried to illustrate through the last few chapters, partnership in Business-to-Business Software-as-a-Service (SaaS) requires significant effort – much more than these examples. This effort must be aimed at building relationships on a foundation of trust, the same approach you would take in your personal life. Those relationships and that trust are designed to create an environment for the customer where they experience more value than any of the single parties could provide alone.

Of course, ecosystems are also designed to build an environment that benefits the individual partners – and benefits them in a big way. Data shows that deals involving one or more partners close faster and at a higher average contract value. They are also stickier, meaning they have a higher lifetime value than those deals without a partner present. For individuals who are compensated based on the achievement of those goals, sellers such as myself, that provides a huge personal benefit, alongside the obvious company-level rewards.

When working directly with Marketo, their partner leadership would continually advertise to their sellers that working deals with partners yielded on average . . .

- Twice the average selling price
- 172% increase in pipeline creation
- 270% increase in customer lifetime value

Think about that for a minute. By tapping into trusted relationships, you effectively double some of the most impactful metrics in a healthy SaaS business.

With these stats as the backdrop, let's go behind the curtain to see what this looks like from the ground level, when it all goes right.

Building Trust and Value in Adobe's Changing Ecosystem

By 2021, Marketo had been acquired by Adobe, and we'd gone through the third iteration of fundamentally rebuilding our partnership in the wake of similar changes. Each transition brought change in the organization, change in leadership, change in the partner program, and change in the field. It was our job to continually identify the best targets, build, and rebuild our relationships within Adobe.

Members of the original Marketo team were now scattered across the organization in a variety of roles. We could still leverage some, but not others. The single constant was continuing to activate the areas of the field organization to whom we could provide the most value. One such opportunity resided in one of their mid-market sales teams that had a pretty juicy patch. Because the Adobe customer base was so large, many of the sellers were required to make a move up market from the size of prospect they had previously sold to.

This particular team, prior to the acquisition, had been selling Marketo into what at the time was considered mid-market companies ($50 million to $500 million in annual revenue). That segment was now considered small business at Adobe, and therefore the new segment they were aligned to were companies with $500 million to $4 billion in annual revenue. What's more, their territories included only accounts without the presence of any other Adobe products. This is significant for a few reasons:

- Enterprise-like cycle: Companies in that revenue range begin to require a true enterprise sales cycle, meaning larger buying committees, a focus on demonstrable value, and added red tape.
- Accounts with no Adobe products:
  - Without the presence of other Adobe products, even if they had sold Marketo for the highest possible price, this team's accounts would never qualify as a key accounts. This meant no assignment of key account resources, and therefore this team was on an island. They did not have the support of Adobe account managers or sales engineers to open doors or build value engineering models.
  - This also meant that this segment was likely a group of late adopters. Adobe has a massive product and customer footprint; companies of that size with zero Adobe product presence were likely more traditional, less tech-forward companies.

For us, it meant we had the opportunity to support a team of younger sellers, who had not sold enterprise-like deals in their past. We could offer them value engineering, third-party validation, and the skill sets necessary to facilitate true digital transformation within a market segment ripe for growth change. Starting in 2020 and into 2021, my partner sales efforts were focused squarely on building relationships with this team.

A New Approach to Objection Handling

In September 2020, I received a call from one of the account executives (AEs) on this team. He told me that he'd just gotten off a call with a $2 billion wholesale packaging distributor out of Chicago. They seemed interested in true digital marketing transformation, inclusive of adopting marketing automation software, potentially Marketo. However, given that they were a Microsoft partner and customer, it would be incredibly challenging to bring in a platform outside of the Microsoft technology suite, even if the alternative was a superior solution.

Astutely, this AE recalled one of the many objection-handling triggers I had pounded into their heads for months, which was our ability to provide third-party validation. As such, he suggested that they speak with a partner to evaluate their needs and determine if Marketo was a solution actually worth exploring. Think about that for a minute. A software sales rep relinquished control of a prospect, allowing them to meet with a partner independently, in order to determine if he had the right to sell them his product. Unheard of!

That was the level of trust that we built with this team. I'm sure it was extremely difficult to hand over an interested prospect, knowing full well we might tell that prospect that in fact Marketo was not a good fit. Ultimately, he did what was in the best interest of the customer and therefore ultimately himself – which I'll unpack.

That first call with the prospect was with their information technology (IT) manager, which was an atypical entry point for Marketo. She had a lot of questions about the marketing automation ecosystem, Marketo, and how it fit into the Microsoft ecosystem. My job was to listen and poke around a bit, trying to uncover what they were ultimately trying to accomplish. It turned out that the company benefited greatly from the pandemic; their net new customer acquisition growth, along with expansion revenues from current customers, hit all-time highs. As a result, their board set an edict to capitalize on the digital trends that had sparked this growth and further improve on their already record growth for the next fiscal year.

The IT manager oversaw their technology stack (which was 98% Microsoft) along with the evaluation of new technology solutions. I used this opportunity to guide her technology approach by conducting discovery about their underlying Go-to-Market (GTM) strategy and its ability to support the growth goals the executives had put into their annual plan.

I knew these areas were not under her purview, but my questions would ultimately guide her to the realization that it would be necessary to involve marketing leadership to effectively perform the evaluation she was tasked with. She proceeded to facilitate a call between me and the senior vice president (SVP) of marketing.

After my initial calls with the prospect, it was critical that I continue to build the relationship with the AE over at Marketo. This meant talking through the call with him, sharing what I learned, and discussing how we wanted to run the deal moving forward. We both agreed this one was going to take some time, and that there was a fair amount of education and buy-in needed from the entire buying group in order for it to materialize as a "real deal."

Establishing Credibility in the Sales Process

We decided that I was going to lead the full discovery process, given the need for a third-party perspective. We'd communicate this to the prospect directly, letting them know that my role moving forward would be to help them evaluate fit for Marketo. There is so much trust baked into making this happen, but because I had established a relationship on the front end, here is what the Marketo AE knew:

- This prospect might never turn into a legitimate sales opportunity unless we stepped in to help him explicitly demonstrate value rather than features and functions of software.

- He didn't have the resources on his team to run a full value engineering engagement with this group as a presales activity.

- My request is to always bring me in early. It's never too early to build a relationship, and often that relationship is core to changing the buyer's perceptions from a simple technology purchase into a planning process for growth. This can overcome hurdles, like the Microsoft hurdle in this deal.

Given that backdrop, we communicated to the prospect that I would be taking the lead on the conversations moving forward. By doing so, the Marketo AE built a tremendous amount of credibility and trust with the prospect by showing that he was willing to walk away and let someone else determine the fate of the deal. From then on, my job was to educate, probe, and determine the best path forward for this group, all while keeping my partner (the Marketo AE) up-to-date with information, and also ensuring he didn't freak out.

The next call with the prospect included the SVP of marketing. A dynamic leader who'd been in the space for some time, she knew the expectations of the board were going to be tough to achieve by simply "running it back." The organic demand from the pandemic was handled in what would be considered a brute force method. There were no systems in place to capture and process the increased demand; it was done by people in a very manual way.

Additionally, there weren't systems in place to generate demand on a go-forward basis. On top of that, this business would be considered by many to be a traditional, or *old school*, business. It was ripe for disruption and, like many other organizations we had helped, they had been forced to rapidly adopt digital GTM channels as a result of the pandemic that now needed to be optimized or even re-implemented.

My next conversations revealed even more about the organization and, more importantly, revealed a lot about this leader's personal motivations. She wanted to leave an imprint on the company, lead them into the digital age, and play a key role in their future growth. At the same time, she was acutely aware of the uphill battle she would face bringing in new technologies to assist in that transformation.

As we were reminded several times throughout the process by the IT manager, it's considered a risk to bring in technology outside of the Microsoft ecosystem and it represents a significant increase in spend to do so. Their status with Microsoft offered them deep discounts on what would be considered as competitive products to Marketo.

Crafting a Comprehensive Business Case

With that backdrop, we began to map out what it would take to transform this organization, with a marketing automation platform like Marketo as the centerpiece. We'd need to define and map use cases to functions, establish current performance benchmarks, and design a fully baked strategy, process, and staffing plan that provided a significant lift in performance above and beyond what they'd get from Microsoft. On top of all of this, the new technologies would need to seamlessly integrate with their preexisting systems and processes. No small feat.

Pulling this all together would require at least a dozen cross-functional deep dives with their team to pull data, understand how that information worked, and translate that into a business case driven implementation plan that would ultimately need to be presented to the board for approval. It takes a strong commitment from both parties to embark on such a journey, and getting that buy-in from the prospect was critical. All parties present committed to the process, which was a huge step in the right direction.

At this point, it was equally important to update our partner and set a sales game plan. I provided the backdrop of the call and committed to him that I would take on the responsibility of the deep dives with their team to understand how they work and uncover the true business opportunity.

What I needed from him was to operate in the background to guide me as to how Marketo's technology would handle the required use cases and also how it would integrate with the prospect's workflows within the existing Microsoft systems. I would use what I received from him as key levers in the business case we'd be building with them.

The other piece we rallied around was, of course, actually getting this deal done in a reasonable time frame. We needed a target to shoot for, and decided that it was wise to leverage their mid-Q2 board meeting as the backstop for presenting the business case to the board of directors. This would provide enough time for pricing and legal approvals while still allowing us the runway necessary to get the deal closed by the end of Q2.

Securing Buy-In and Conducting Discovery

The next call with the prospect where the Marketo AE and I both attended, we made a point to get full buy-in on the plan we created. That included acceptance of the Q2 board meeting as our compelling event, where the green light would be granted to push this deal forward. We obtained our buyer's approval on the entire plan early in that call, and then we proceeded to identify everyone in the organization who would attend the discovery sessions we needed to conduct over the next couple of months. That looked like the following people and meetings:

- Lead data analyst, who walked me through how they track, measure, and define performance
- IT manager, who provided a deep dive into how the Microsoft ecosystem was built
- Marketing operations manager, who talked me through the workflows for lead management, processing, and handoffs to sales
- Sales manager, who provided a download on how they sell, assets they use, and the overarching sales process
- SVP of marketing, who took me through the entire GTM strategy from end to end

These discovery sessions occurred over a two-month period in which I gathered inputs that would help me construct the detailed business case for this project. Additionally, with each conversation I'd identify use cases that would act as strategic levers to drive ROI for the business. I would then feed Marketo those outputs so they could provide me functional ammunition to augment the business case.

It took me about a month to build the initial straw-man for master plan, which became the backbone of each conversation with the SVP of marketing from that point forward. I needed her buy-in on this approach, so we would design and iterate on the business case together. As we needed technical gaps filled, we would pull in the Marketo AE for demos, screenshots, and validation of what we designed. This was all very intentionally coordinated to ensure that we were building something that would perform in the real world.

Preparing for the Board Meeting

About the time the business case was hardened, the board meeting was in our sights. The full ROI model was simply too much for a board meeting, so I worked with the SVP of marketing to distill it down to brass tacks, clear, easy to consume visuals. That meant trimming down 43 slides of content to 10.

This wasn't easy; making the complex simple is always a challenge, but it was a necessity for this audience, and squarely the value engineering role I had signed up to fulfill. A few rounds of revisions, a couple of practice calls later, and we sent our champion off to the board meeting with the fate of the entire project in her hands. A few notes on what was included in the business case:

- The business goal, recommendation, and the ask – right off the bat

- Functional business improvements achieved by the plan, validated by their team
- Financial "lift" model based on their benchmarks in their language
- Full Return on investment (ROI) analysis including Marketo software costs and LeadMD services costs included
- Repeat of the goal, the ROI, the ask, with the addition of the required commitment timeline followed by next steps

You can access our framework for developing world class, value-centric business cases for sales by visiting the following QR code:.

Figure 12.1 shows an image of the ROI model that was included in the business case described previously.

We got the buy-in we needed from the board, including the commitment to sign the deal with both Marketo and LeadMD once the implementation plan was finalized. Great news! We had three weeks to produce the implementation plan and for Marketo to align their sales order with what had been presented.

	Current State Assumptions	Targets	Lead Conversion Rate	Prospect Conversion Rate	Close Rate	Expansion Revenue	Conservative Lift All Levers	Aggressive Lift All Levers
Targets	22,000	33,000	22,000	22,000	22,000	22,000	33,000	35,200
Lead Conversion Rate	49%	49%	52%	49%	49%	49%	52%	54%
Leads	10700	16,170	11,440	10,780	10,780	10,780	17,160	19,008
Prospect Conversion Rate	22%	22%	22%	25%	22%	22%	25%	27%
Prospects	2373	3,557	2,517	2,695	2,372	2,372	4,290	5,132
NNA Close Rate	19%	19%	19%	19%	20%	19%	20%	22%
New Name Accounts	399	676	478	512	474	451	858	1,129
New Name Account 1st Year GPS '18-'20	$2,381,049	$4,033,497	$2,853,631	$3,055,680	$2,830,524	$2,688,998	$5,120,150	$6,737,803
Average Deal Size (GPS) - Year 1	$5,968	$5,968	$5,968	$5,968	$5,968	$5,968	$5,968	$5,968
Expansion Rate	300%	300%	300%	300%	300%	325%	325%	350%
3 Year Expansion GPS	$7,343,795	$12,100,491	$8,560,892	$9,167,039	$8,491,573	$8,739,244	$16,640,489	$23,582,310
TOTAL GPS	$9,724,844	$16,133,988	$11,414,522	$12,222,718	$11,322,097	$11,428,242	$21,760,640	$30,320,113
Potential Lift in GPS		$6,409,144	$1,689,678	$2,497,874	$1,597,253	$1,703,398	$12,035,796	$30,320,113

Adopting Marketo/Lead MD will lead to 124% growth over 3 years

Figure 12.1 The business use case.
Source: Copyright In Review Capital.

The Stakes Get Higher

I must take a little step back here to provide some insight into what was happening in the background at LeadMD while this process occurred. As the foundation of the deal was coming together, I was coordinating with our internal consulting services teams who ultimately would deliver on this project, on top of all the coordination I was doing externally.

I had been working with one of our principals, which is what we called the leaders within our consulting practice, for the duration of the two-month business case process. Together we had begun organizing resources for this project, validating delivery capabilities with functional requirements, and ultimately building the implementation plan that would be our guide to ensure we delivered on our promise.

That principal was my internal partner in assembling a scope of work, ensuring that the approach we formulated, and ultimately proposed, was going to produce the desired results for the prospect. Principals also played another important role, one responsible for instilling confidence in the would-be buyer that this plan was not simply being designed by a couple of overzealous sales guys from Marketo and LeadMD; rather, it was rooted in best practices and assembled by experts, who were ultimately responsible for delivering success.

We spent the next three weeks leading up to our close date iterating on the implementation plan, ensuring not only that we had the resources aligned to the project but also that the prospect had their team and expectations aligned as well. There was a lot at stake here. Our champion was not willing to leave anything to chance, given her very reputation within the organization was on the line. This project had to succeed.

Sealing the Deal

As these things tend to do, despite intricate planning, the deal still came down to the wire. While we were finalizing the implementation plan, agreements had been sent to legal for review. That process took slightly longer than anticipated, which led to last-minute negotiations with legal about contract terms on the very last day of the quarter. Not ideal.

At one point, it seemed the deal might even slip into the next quarter because, coincidentally, all three parties to the agreement (myself, the Marketo AE, and the buyer) were traveling that day. Lo and behold, enabled by the power of airport Wi-Fi and a bit of give-and-take by everyone involved, we had a finalized contract, out for electronic signature, which was ultimately executed within 15 minutes of receipt at 7:30 p.m. Down to the wire indeed.

When it all goes right, you have a partnership built on trust. Doing the things you want a true partner to do. The most simple definition of value in a partner co-sell deal is of course the deal itself. For Marketo, it was a 24-month software commitment for $250 000 in annual recurring revenue with no discounting. This was unheard of at this point in SaaS sales. For LeadMD, this meant a $300 000 total contract value that included implementation and annually recurring managed services.

The true value of this partner co-selling process was the fact that this sales opportunity would never have existed without the parties coming together in the way they did. The prospect would have purchased another cog in the Microsoft stack, because without engaging a partner, the entire value engineering process would have been absent. The win was built on value communicated through the business case – not features and functionality – real value built by a partner.

More important, by bringing us into the deal very early, we were able to build a plan based on the customer's true business goals, not simply implementing technology, which generally yielded a much lower contract value for us.

In contrast to the story shared about when it all goes wrong, you are serving your customer better *and* delivering better revenue results for your organization when it all goes right.

Chapter 13

Insights into Successful Partner Programs

Sean Kester
Partner, In Revenue Capital

As a partner at In Revenue Capital, I'm all-in on the power of partnership programs. This belief isn't new; I've embraced it firsthand through many years of work with startups and Business-to-Business organizations. Here's a look at my journey, along with some takeaways that might be useful to you in yours.

Partnership at Salesloft

When I joined Salesloft as one of the first employees, I was tasked with building the sales development team. From there, I moved on to building out the product organization. While doing so, we identified that our product was at the center of our customers' workflow and had the opportunity to become a platform.

Early on, I recognized that we could integrate other technologies into our platform and create an ecosystem other partners would build into, meeting our joint customers where they were already living. This realization was crucial for developing a successful partnership ecosystem.

We decided to open up application programming interfaces (APIs) for third-party integrations, creating an ecosystem around our technology. This included robust app directories, developer documentation, integration, and marketing support programs. We also enabled internal teams to understand our partners' products and presented our platform to their teams, fostering a collaborative, co-selling environment where combining our solutions created greater value.

The early creation of an app ecosystem became one of the strongest competitive differentiators in our market. Because we could anticipate our customers' needs years ahead of the competition, we leveraged our robust ecosystem of partners, integrations, and combined workflows to consistently differentiate and win against our competitors.

> **Note:** It's important to note that establishing partnerships within the business wasn't as easy as it might sound. Some teams were large enough to have an executive leader, but everyone had their own priorities. This meant that integrating partnerships as a strategic arm of the business took a long time and required a lot of effort.
>
> We often had to push initiatives forward, even if some weren't on board initially. For example, we implemented programs to build co-selling motions with our partners despite internal resistance, needing to prove their value through return on investment (ROI), which was difficult early on.

Finding the Balance Between Partnerships and Sales

Partnerships differ from sales in that, although their importance is recognized, demonstrating direct ROI isn't always cut and dried. In a traditional sales motion, the ROI is clear: hire salespeople with quotas, and you'll see returns. Marketing also shows direct ROI: invest in ads, and you get measurable returns. However, partnerships involve softer metrics like influencing deals, co-selling, and referrals, which can be harder to quantify and predict in advance.

Given all this, convincing the executive team to view partnerships as a viable Go-to-Market (GTM) channel was tougher than advocating for direct sales. This is a common struggle across organizations. The few exceptions are those with CEOs or executive team members with a partnership background and prioritizing partnership strategies through the GTM organizations.

Ultimately, it's all about finding the right balance between partnerships and more traditional strategies to drive business growth effectively.

Adopting a Partner Ecosystem Strategy

Many organizations have adopted a partnership model, which is often referred to as a partner ecosystem *strategy*. This enables them to test new products, services, price points, or markets more cost-effectively by collaborating with partners rather than hiring and training new sales teams. Finding a channel partner or another market ally is generally cheaper and quicker than expanding internally.

To succeed, it's essential to get executive buy-in. Building these partnerships takes time and doesn't yield immediate results like direct sales, but it can be more effective in the long run. For instance, developing a partner program enhanced Salesloft's branding, market reach, and deal influence, though delivering direct revenue took a bit longer.

As the program matured, we expanded from only a technology/ecosystem partner program to the addition of a solutions partner program, which included referrals, revenue share, and co-selling, and was progressing toward reselling.

To manage the increasing number of customers, we partnered with agencies and consultancies for product implementation. We trained these partners and shared implementation fees, enabling them to offer additional services. This strategy solved our onboarding challenges and expanded our value proposition, creating a network of alliance partners.

These partners not only assisted with implementation but also brought in new business. They recommended our software to clients, establishing a new revenue channel. This success caught the executive team's attention and led to further investment in partnership programs.

We also developed a program with venture capital and private equity firms, offering services and best practices to their portfolio companies. This included webinars, workshops, and discounted access to our platform. This initiative strengthened our market position and ultimately led to one of our partners, Vista, acquiring our company, Salesloft, for several billion dollars. This strategy of building a robust partnership ecosystem enhanced our revenue and paved the way for significant business growth and acquisition.

Creating Successful Partnerships

Finding organizations that can mutually grow value is crucial to forming solid partnerships. On the product side, we formed relationships for co-selling with companies offering complementary products within the same budget and decision-making scope as ours. By coordinating our sales teams, we could co-sell, share accounts, and offer combined discounts, enhancing value for customers.

Aligning customer success teams also played a significant role, though it required substantial effort. Establishing a partnership is just the beginning; ensuring everyone in the organization, from frontline sellers to support staff, understands and prioritizes the partnership is essential. This involves clear communication of objectives, tracking methods, contact points, issue escalation processes, pricing, packaging, and logging details.

The effort required is often underestimated. Each team member has different priorities, and the partnership can falter without proper incentives and executive buy-in. Executives must drive the process changes needed for success because their support ensures alignment and prioritization across all levels. A partnership will only thrive if both sides are committed and coordinated from the top down.

Starting at the Top

To achieve success in partnerships, you need to start at the top. Align with your counterpart, like the vice president of sales, marketing, or customer success, and develop a joint proposal. Ensure both executive teams are on board; without their agreement, progress is impossible.

Once the executives are aligned, distribute the information to the next level – the daily operations teams. This is often where priorities clash and the process stalls. So after securing their alignment, create programs to align frontline teams and reps interacting with customers. It's crucial to communicate clearly from the top down to prevent misunderstandings and ensure everyone understands the initiative's importance.

Experience teaches that proving ROI is difficult, so aim for quick, tangible wins early on, especially in startups where every decision has significant repercussions. For example, partner with a company specializing in enterprise sales instead of building an enterprise sales team from scratch. This approach allows for faster validation and success, ensuring your teams are aligned and ready. If the partnership proves successful, you can consider adding your own sales team later, but starting with partners is often the best way to find initial value.

Trust is crucial to building partnerships, especially for reps involved in co-selling or channel sales. You need to be hyper-vigilant about every interaction on both sides. Positive interactions lead to productive relationships, and negative ones can undermine trust and effort. As such, it's important to overcommunicate expectations and outcomes, and address any issues promptly. If reps experience negative interactions, they might not voice their concerns but will quietly disengage, leading to the partnership's failure.

Define what success looks like, outline roles and responsibilities, and implement checks and balances. Regularly conduct forecasting and pipeline calls to keep everyone on track. Be the stabilizing force when things go wrong and work quickly to resolve issues.

Co-Selling in Practice

An example of co-selling highlights the importance of trust and clear communication. We had a co-selling partnership with another company we integrated with, offering discounts if buyers purchased both products within 30 days. Both sides agreed to these terms.

However, during one particular co-selling motion, our partner miscommunicated, claiming the buyer was committed to moving forward with both solutions when they were not, leading us to give a discount prematurely. This resulted in a loss of trust and strained the partnership. Our executives were upset, and it took significant effort to rebuild the relationship and establish new checks and balances to prevent future issues.

Effective conflict management skills are essential in such scenarios. This is why overcommunicating expectations and being explicit about roles and responsibilities are necessary. In partnerships, disagreements over compensation and credit can arise, especially in co-selling or reseller arrangements. Clearly defined rules of engagement and ownership are necessary to prevent conflicts and ensure smooth operations. For instance, if one of our reps talks to a lead first, they should get credit, not the partner who engaged later.

Building a successful partnership program involves setting up an entire discipline within the company. It requires alignment across all functions – development, product, sales, marketing, customer success, and finance. As a partnership leader, you must ensure everyone is on the same page and pull the right strings without pushing too hard in one area.

Creating a sense of urgency and maintaining executive buy-in is vital. Programs can easily get deprioritized, so you must continuously demonstrate their value. This role often involves more relationship and people management than direct production. Key responsibilities include regular check-ins, nurturing relationships, and addressing issues promptly.

171

Final Thoughts

Partnerships are among the most powerful, largely untapped resources available today, but they require great intentionality and keen acumen. You must build trust and be diligent about clear communication, conflict management, and a holistic approach to integration across all business functions.

Introduce the new partnership process with the understanding that it requires a different skill set and level of trust compared to regular sales. It's a paradigm shift that needs careful management. Additionally, overcommunicate any wins to build momentum and trust in the partnership. Share case studies and examples of successful collaborations to encourage others to participate. Highlight successes to ensure that positive news outweighs any negative experiences.

Finally, recognize that sales reps have many responsibilities, so make partnering as seamless and rewarding as possible to keep them engaged and motivated.

Chapter 14

Cash in Time

Justin Gray and Josh Wagner

We started this book saying, "you've been lied to." This referred to a concept we called the *digital mask*, but, as it turns out, you have been fed yet another untruth. This one might not be so unintentional, and it resides in the traditional Venture capital (VC) model.

This model is built on the success of one and the failure of many, a model built on fund dynamics rather than fundamentals, a model designed to make investors rich and founders less so. The In Revenue Capital model is built with partnership at the center of it, with relationships as a Go-to-Market (GTM) accelerator and a catalyst for successful exit.

The Fallacy of the Traditional Venture Model

The traditional venture model leads you to believe the typical life cycle of a business consists of a series of fundraising rounds, mapped to valuation increases, and conforms to a standard set of milestone-defined metrics. It also tells you that an initial public offering (IPO) is the ultimate validation. But in reality, 80%[1] of successful startup exits are acquisitions, not IPOs. Year over year, we are seeing IPOs decline.[2]

The truth is the lengthy venture journey where taking a company public is the only acceptable off-ramp is a very high-risk, seldom high-reward endeavor. Playing this strange game that requires capital infusion beginning with early seed investment and progressing through an alphabet soup of subsequent, and increasingly dilutive, financings on the hopes of achieving a billion-dollar valuation and IPO, is extremely rare. This route, which has been made out to be the standard by big VC, is anything but. The big venture firms push this narrative because it's the only way *they* can truly make money.

Fund dynamics are an incredibly powerful and dangerous driver in the traditional venture model. As venture firms raise larger and larger funds, the ability to return capital on that sum of money at an outsized return becomes increasingly difficult. They must see $1 billion+ exits to generate the 50–100× returns their limited partners desire. Therein lies the problem.

Billion-dollar valuations are hard to come by, not to mention that valuation ultimately materializing into a liquidity event. With the odds stacked against them for the big exit, they deploy capital under the premise that 1 in 10 investments will hit – and hit big. The model typically looks like 5 of 10 losses: 3 singles that cover their fees, 1 with a 20–50× return that covers their losses, and 1 grand slam with a 100× return or better. This is all over a 10-year projected horizon, as you can see in Figure 14.1.

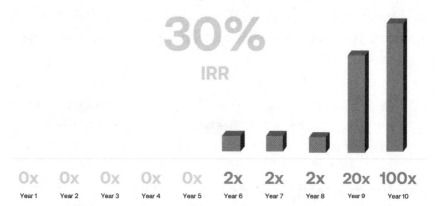

Figure 14.1 Power Law and fund dynamics. *Source:* Copyright In Revenue Capital.

So, what are fund dynamics? Simply put, they are the forces that lead to the evaluation of an investment based not on its own merits but instead on its potential to return 100% or more of the fund's value. This is known as Power Law, a principle that dictates a small number of investments will be responsible for generating a disproportionate amount of the fund's returns. This is a proven principle, but it also reinforces biases that are self-perpetuating. If you look at Power Law and the fund dynamics it creates through the eyes of a startup founder, hopefully, you can see the problem.

The fact that 80% of successful exits are actually acquisitions that take place earlier in a company's life cycle, rather than becoming a unicorn IPO, runs counter to most VC logic and therefore you can conclude a few things:

- Traditional venture is not even looking at most companies out there that could be ripe for M&A (Mergers and acquisitions) activity.
- VC can easily overlook entire cohorts, such as women, minorities, and niche markets, due to risk bias.

175

Cash in Time

- Startups in the portfolio that do not make early traction are quickly tossed aside when it's clear they are not going to meet the outsized expectations.

- Founders who do make it *all the way* under this model are often diluted down to less than 5% ownership of "their" company, making a lot of other people very rich, while they are left with very little to show for their efforts.

The Partnership Model

You might be thinking, "What does all of this have to do with partnerships?" We're getting there. Let us get back to acquisition as the primary vehicle for many successful exits. First, we should define what a successful exit is. However, that element should truly be defined by the founder.

Instead, it's often defined by capital providers, whether that's what the founder wants or not, simply because venture math is so pervasive. Thanks to this perpetuated narrative, founders have been trained to pander to this outcome above all else.

My favorite question to ask a founder in an early conversation is, "What do you want to get out of this business?" You'd think it would be an easy question for them to answer, but I find they end up struggling, "Do I tell them what I think they want to hear, or do I tell them what I actually want?" This tends to lead to a very "vanilla" answer, lacking inspiration. Not what you want to hear from a founder with whom you are potentially investing millions of dollars!

The reality is that an outcome generating, say, $10 million of cash for the founder sets the stage for life-changing wealth. Although $10 million is a far cry from $1 billion, it's certainly a lot of money and is a result that can be achieved more reliably and with far fewer headaches than the pursuit of creating a public company. A path with less fundraising, less dilution, and more focus on the customer, and the key to doing so can again be found through partnerships.

Partnerships Can Lead to Acquisitions

Let us look at the differences between an exit through acquisition versus an IPO. The traditional venture model needs a $1 billion valuation or more to generate enough value in the business for the VC to meet their goals, not the founder's. The acquisition path has the potential to create wealth faster and more effectively for the founder while still generating excellent returns, in the case that there are outside investors on the capitalization table.

The traditional venture path is driven by the exponential increase in valuation as the business grows and meets goals. The problem with that model is that, as the valuation increases with each round, the share price is based on that valuation, and the pool of potential buyers shrinks. The number of prospective acquirers at a $10 million valuation is drastically larger than the amount at a $100 million valuation and so on.

There are simply fewer companies large enough to make that type of deal. As a founder looking to take in capital, it's critical to think about the impact of the valuation of your funding round compared to the outcome you are looking to achieve. If we go back to the $10 million cash outcome for a founder, there is a good chance you need to build a company worth at least $20 million in enterprise value to meet that cash objective.

This backdrop is intended to set the stage for how we evaluate partnerships through the lens of potential M&A. There are hundreds of examples of companies being acquired by their largest partner, as shown in Figure 14.2.

COMPANY	ACQUIRER/PARTNER	YEAR	AMOUNT
GitHub	Microsoft	2018	$7.5 billion
Slack Technologies	Salesforce	2021	$27.7 billion
Tableau Software	Salesforce	2019	$15.7 billion
Qualtrics	SAP	2019	$8 billion
MuleSoft	Salesforce	2018	$6.5 billion
Momentive (formerly SurveyMonkey)	Zendesk	2023	$4 billion
Brandfolder	Smartsheet	2022	$155 billion
Ultimate Software	Hellman & Friedman and Blackstone	2020	$11 billion
npm (Node Package Manager)	GitHub	2020	–
Mindville	Atlassian	2020	–

Figure 14.2 Service-as-a-Software (SaaS) acquisitions by partners. *Source:* Copyright In Revenue Capital.

Partnership is our Cheat Code for GTM because it's the shortest path to trust; the same can be said in the M&A discussion. Companies do not blindly make acquisitions. You've likely heard that it's all about the numbers at the end of the day, but that's not completely true. It might come down to the numbers once you are in the conversation, but how do you start the conversation?

Microsoft, a company that drives 95% of its revenue through partnership, is not acquiring just any company out there that "meets the metrics." They are strategically acquiring partners who have made an outsized impact on their business, which begin to make more sense inside the business than outside. This thinking should fundamentally change how you evaluate fundraising, capital partners, and your GTM partners.

Using a tactical example, we invested in a company with a very strong partner ecosystem, which was obviously a critical point in our investment thesis. Post-investment, we were evaluating where we should focus our GTM partner effort. Pre-investment, we aligned with this founder and determined their desired outcome was exit via acquisition in three to five years. Having that alignment helped us to focus on partnership through another dimension – exit potential.

Turns out, of the top two partners:

- Partner 1 had made three acquisitions in the past 10 years, with a strong propensity to build versus buy.
- Partner 2 had made 23 acquisitions in the past 10 years, with a strong propensity to buy versus build.

All GTM partner profiling aside, partner 2 was a much better strategic fit from a pure exit perspective. Historically, if you can acquire a substantive number of their customers, it's enough to get the attention of their executive team for M&A talk. Acquisition potential as a data point is an important dimension in ideal partner profiling efforts.

Another company in our portfolio is focused on health care. It turns out that in addition to several technology companies that share the same ICP, there are also a good number of consulting firms that explicitly focus on their specialty, making them a natural fit as a GTM partner. Again, if we add the lens of acquisition potential, an outcome pre-vetted with the founder, we have another filter through which to prioritize partnership.

This space has dozens of consulting firms from small boutique players to very large private equity–backed players. We evaluated all potential partners through the lens of acquisition appetite; as it turns out, two emerged as large enough to acquire, one of which was private equity backed and the other employee owned. The private equity–backed organization had a history of M&A activity that shaped our GTM efforts. In that instance, both parties acknowledged the fact that this partnership would open the doors to those conversations.

At the end of the day, acquisition should not be the only focus of a partnership but an additional dimension to consider when evaluating potential partners. A word to the wise: do not put all your eggs in one basket, as they say. The M&A view of partnership is an important one, but the goal should be twofold:

- Create outsized enterprise value for the business.
- Create optionality for yourself as it pertains to exit potential.

When cash-in time comes, and you are looking to create wealth for yourself (instead of making a VC firm rich), partnership is your Cheat Code.

How It Works in Practice

These theories always sound great in promise, but do they hold up in practice? The truth is, we would not be writing this book today if they had not had both a practical as well as a profound impact on our personal journeys. As mentioned toward the start of this book, I've (Justin) been fortunate enough to create and build five successful companies and enjoy exits from all of them by fundamentally leveraging these strategies. The most recent of these exits occurred in 2021, and by that time, I had the benefit of context from the previous four.

In each case, the exit came through either a critical strategic partnership or a line of sight obtained by the acquirer as a by-product of those relationships. Often, this was due to the fact that our strategic partners had a much larger public brand than our own, and hence their interest amplified market interest as a result.

However, that 2021 acquisition (the acquisition of LeadMD) was truly a culmination of these strategies honed over time and deployed in a highly intentional manner. To highlight these, we need to hop in the way-back machine to somewhere in the 2010 time frame.

I had always known the LeadMD story was a finite one. In truth, when you speak to almost any founder who has created and run a services business, they will attest to the fact that it is a very difficult business model – and for many, the worst. Businesses in which the product is, quite literally, people, for many in private capital allocation, are considered to be the kiss of death.

Far removed from the handsome revenue multiples attached to SaaS darlings, service revenues are not only less attractive to many acquirers but also, inversely, software organizations are actively discouraged from building service offerings by advisors and investors alike. All of this to say, they are incredibly difficult to scale.

At LeadMD's inception, I knew all of this. Even though I was coming off the success of my first exit, it was not an "island and a boat" exit, meaning I still very much needed to work. It did allow me the runway to create several of my own businesses without the stress of worrying about immediate income. Make no mistake, however; the time horizon on that runway was a stressor in and of itself. Hence, my creation of LeadMD, a marketing consulting firm, was born out of necessity as well as proximity.

I needed to make use of the marketable assets I possessed, and at that time, that was GTM and marketing technology expertise. As such, the product was set. I knew we could capture the market by filling a critical need, given the birth of digital marketing technologies, but I did not know how far we could take it. So, I set a lofty revenue and Earnings Before Interest, Taxes, Depreciation, and Amortization (EBITDA) goal, and was off to the races deploying all of the tactics we have outlined in this book to do so.

By 2018, we had exceeded all of those early performance goals, and by a factor of two. This was the first time I considered we might have been nearing the end of the journey. Something at that time just did not feel right as we were still firing on all cylinders, and I had plenty of fight left in me. I had started LeadMD at the beginning of a major recession, but after navigating the global pandemic, the wild swings that define a professional services business were finally starting to take their toll.

Despite the global shutdown, we had seen even more increased growth during COVID-19 and had a very impressive decade of software-esque performance in our rearview mirror. Everything seemed to point toward a very attractive time to exit. Even with those strong signals, I do not know if I would have been as bullish on a sale as I was had it not been for the acquisition of one of our strongest strategic partners, TOPO.

TOPO was a Business-to-Business SaaS research and advisory firm with whom we had successfully partnered for years. Our businesses had incredibly beneficial concentric circles, as we were not only aligned in methodology but also had almost no competitive overlap. Our clients were theirs and vice versa. Even more beneficial was the fact that the more a client consumed of either offering, the even greater fit they were for the other.

Scott Albro and Craig Rosenberg, the founders and principals of TOPO, were good friends of mine. In fact, Craig has been one of my most cherished mentors for more than a decade, so when they shared that they were considering an acquisition – and a handsome one at that – my ears perked up.

Once the deal had been closed and was announced, I spent a good deal of time with them reviewing the process they had gone through, the expectations that could be garnered and ultimately, how they finally came to the decision to sell. I was ready to dip my toe in the water, albeit a very strategic toe. I wanted to ensure that word did not get out and that we would only consider the transaction if the acquisition would greatly bolster the value of the company and the lives of our employees.

TOPO had leveraged an investment banking group to facilitate and broker the transaction, and, as I find with most things, they communicated that the success of the deal ultimately came down to *who* they had worked with at the firm. As someone who goes around exalting concepts like "relationships are the currency of success," this was music to my ears – and it began the journey of what would consume the next six months of my life.

Craig and Scott ultimately brokered an introduction to the two bankers who had been brokered their transaction. It just so happens that in the period between their deal closing and my outreach, they had left the big recognizable shop they had been with for many years to strike out on their own and hang a shingle. Now, I think this might have been a turnoff for many; after all, who wants to be the inaugural client of a very green firm when so much is on the line?

LeadMD had always been my baby; our employees were incomparable and it's hard not to be romantic about a company built by so much consistent hard work and ingenuity. And yet, I never gave the newly minted nature of their firm a second thought. The banking partner had the ringing endorsement of two very trusted partners (and friends) and that context was all I needed to jump in with both feet.

Over the years, I had many conversations with potential acquirers of LeadMD. One such offer had even come prior to the opening of our doors from who would become one of our primary competitors. Early on, I always viewed our software partners as the most likely acquirers, given our incredibly close relationship with them and their end users. However, by the time we were ready, all of those potential candidates had either been acquired themselves or were more focused on their own IPO dreams.

Still, I do not want to discount the potential for software and services firm courtships. We've seen it time and time again within our ecosystems and even our portfolio. But, when we engaged Brightower, they opened an entirely new aperture on the strategic search. By identifying them through a trusted partner we had circumvented months of undue diligence that in all likelihood would not have yielded a fit anywhere as perfect.

This is the power of relationships, and in this example, it yielded a partner who not only focused on our explicit market but also had the experience and insight necessary to identify a short list of ideal acquirers. They knew who was in market, they knew who had been jilted at the altar before, they knew what we were looking for and where to find it. You hear many horror stories about the sale of closely held companies – partnership helped us avoid all of that here.

We reached out to 10 possibilities and 8 confirmed the timing was right and that our makeup met the criteria they were interested in.

From there, four offers ensued, and we ultimately selected the best one – all in a period of three months.

If that process seems smooth, it's because it was. Now, LeadMD was an incredibly strong business (in fact, I'm still realizing how rare our metrics were) but this process could have easily gone in a different direction. The truth is we had been architecting the success of the transaction for many years before it started by investing in a partner ecosystem that we could rely on and call on for virtually any need. And within those partners were friendships.

That's a whole different chapter, perhaps even a different book. As I look back at the 12 years I spent at the helm of LeadMD, I do not first remember the engagements, or the events, or the problems we overcame. I remember the friendships I still enjoy to this day. I see those people often: the customers, the employees, and the partners that comprise my happiest memories.

There's so much there that transcends business and simply becomes *life*. The financial rewards are truly dwarfed by the value of the relationships I formed – and continue to form. Because of course the story does not end; the setting just changes. In the few years that have passed since LeadMD stopped being that small, scrappy, perpetual startup consultancy out of Arizona, and our former employees have gone on to found their own businesses, taken executive positions at high-performing companies, and even become venture capitalists and investors. These are individuals I speak to often both to exchange advice and also to call on when their skill sets are necessary. They have opened doors for me, and I've been more than happy to do the same for them. Relationships truly are the currency of success, and they are an asset I consider to be one of my most valuable, and certainly the highest performing.

Conclusion

Justin Gray
Josh Wagner

In writing this book, we wanted to bring tangibility and pragmatism to the growth lever of relationships, which for far too long has wallowed in obscurity. We hope this has offered a fresh perspective on how to achieve sustainable growth through the power of strategic partnerships. We hope it's your Cheat Code to win more during a time when the "modern" marketing and sales playbooks are losing their effectiveness. As we conclude this book, let's revisit five key takeaways.

Trust Is the Foundation of Modern B2B Growth

The central thesis of *The Go-to-Market Cheat Code* is that trust, built through genuine relationships, is the most crucial element for sustainable growth. In a market saturated with digital noise and mediocre content, buyers are increasingly turning to trusted sources for recommendations and insights. By fostering authentic relationships, businesses can create a foundation of trust that drives long-term success.

Partnerships as Strategic Growth Levers

Viewing partnerships as mere transactions or sales channels must fundamentally change. Instead, approach partnerships as a strategic, integrated growth lever. Use our playbook for identifying ideal partners, creating joint value propositions, and leveraging these partnerships to achieve mutual success.

A Customer-Centric Approach

A recurring theme in *The Go-to-Market Cheat Code* is the need for a customer-first mindset. We argue that understanding and addressing the needs and goals of the customer should be at the forefront of every strategy. By aligning with partners who share this customer-centric approach, businesses can create a powerful ecosystem that delivers exceptional value and drives growth.

Operationalizing Relationships

Relationships can, like trust, seem ambiguous to define, but we hope the practical steps we've outlined will help you operationalize relationship-based growth. This includes setting up processes to capture customer insights, aligning internal teams on partnership goals, and creating mechanisms to ensure that the value delivered to customers is consistently high.

The Power of a Collaborative Culture

Finally, this book highlights the importance of fostering a collaborative culture within the organization. This involves securing executive buy-in, ensuring that all departments understand the value of partnerships, and embedding a partnership mindset throughout the company. A culture that values collaboration and mutual success is essential for maximizing the impact of strategic relationships.

Moving Forward

As you move forward from reading this book, consider how you can apply these key takeaways to your own business, and even your life. Reflect on your current strategies and identify areas where you can enhance trust, build stronger partnerships, operationalize your relationship-building efforts, and foster a collaborative culture. By doing so, you will be well equipped to navigate the complexities of the modern B2B landscape and achieve not only sustainable growth to outpace your competition but also create relationships that will fuel success in every aspect of your life.

Supplemental Information

Glossary

ABM	Account-Based Marketing	**IPO**	Initial Public Offering
AE	Account Executive	**IPP**	Ideal Partner Profile
CAC	Customer Acquisition Cost	**IT**	Information Technology
CLV	Customer Lifetime Value	**JVP**	Joint Value Proposition
CRM	Customer Relationship Management	**M&A**	Mergers and Acquisitions
CSM	Customer Success Manager	**MQL**	Marketing Qualified Lead
EBITDA	Earnings Before Interest, Taxes, Depreciation, and Amortization	**ROI**	Return on Investment
		SQL	Sales Qualified Lead
		SVP	Senior Vice President
ICP	Ideal Customer Profile	**TOPO**	A B2B SaaS research and advisory firm

Definitions

- **Account-Based Marketing (ABM):** A strategic Go-to-Market approach based on a set of target accounts and their contacts.

- **Account mapping:** The process of aligning sales and marketing efforts with specific accounts.

- **Acquisition:** The process of acquiring control of another company.

- **Churn:** The percentage of customers who stop using a product during a given time period.

- **Customer Acquisition Cost (CAC):** The cost associated with convincing a consumer to buy a product or service.

- **Customer Lifetime Value (CLV):** A metric that estimates how much revenue a customer will generate for a business over the course of their relationship.

- **Customer Relationship Management (CRM):** A technology for managing all your company's relationships and interactions with customers and potential customers.

- **Digital mask:** The flawed concept that digital interaction has changed buyer behavior significantly.

- **Ecosystem:** A complex network or interconnected system.

- **Exit:** Occurs when an investor and/or entrepreneur sells part or all of their ownership in a company, either for profit or at a loss.

- **Inbound marketing:** Marketing strategies that focus on attracting customers through content and interactions that are relevant and helpful.

- **Lead life cycle:** The process of managing leads from generation through conversion to customers.

- **Mergers and Acquisitions (M&A):** Consolidation of companies or assets through various types of financial transactions.

- **Outbound marketing:** Marketing strategies that involve reaching out to potential customers.

- **Partner ecosystem:** A network of strategic partnerships that enhance the offerings of each member.

- **Pipeline:** The sales pipeline; the steps an individual goes through from lead to customer.

- **Referral fee:** A payment made to someone who refers a new customer to a business.

- **Sales engagement:** The interactions that salespeople have with their prospects and customers.

- **Sales process:** A series of steps that are followed by a salesperson to move a prospect from an early stage lead to a closed customer.

- **Sales Qualified Lead (SQL):** A prospective customer who has been researched and vetted by an organization's marketing department and sales team.

- **Strategic partner:** A critical relationship between two commercial enterprises, usually formalized by one or more business contracts.

- **Technographic:** The analysis of the technology used by an organization.

Notes

Chapter 1

1. Gartner: https://www.gartner.com/en/newsroom/press-releases/2020-09-15-gartner-says-80--of-b2b-sales-interactions-between-su.
2. Consultancy & Exact Target: https://searchengineland.com/report-digital-marketing-budgets-to-increase-in-2010-35087; Gartner:. https://www.gartner.com/en/marketing/topics/marketing-budget.

Chapter 2

1. Venkat Atluri and Miklós Dietz, "Strategies to Win in the New Ecosystem Economy," *McKinsey*, August 24, 2023, https://www.mckinsey.com/capabilities/strategy-and-corporate-finance/our-insights/strategies-to-win-in-the-new-ecosystem-economy.
2. Interview from Partnership Leader Catalyst conference in Miami in 2022.
3. Partner Insight, "75% of World Trade Flows Indirectly - Jay McBain @ Forrester (part 1/3)," February 15, 2020, https://www.partnerinsight.io/post/jay-mcbain-forrester-75-of-world-trade-flows-indirectly-pt1-3.
4. Nicole Dezen, "Microsoft Ecosystem Value: New Data Reveals Partner Paths to Profitability and Growth," Microsoft, September 15, 2022, https://partner.microsoft.com/en-US/blog/article/microsoft-ecosystem-value-new-data-reveals-partner-paths-to-profitability-and-growth.
5. Bessemer Venture Partners: "State of the Cloud 2022," https://www.bvp.com/atlas/state-of-the-cloud-2022.

Chapter 5

1. Clayton M. Christensen, Taddy Hall, Karen Dillon, and David S. Duncan, "Know Your Customers' 'Jobs to Be Done,'" *Harvard Business Review*, September 2016, https://hbr.org/2016/09/know-your-customers-jobs-to-be-done#:~:text=In%20a%20recent%20McKinsey%20poll,fall%20far%20short%20of%20ambitions.

Chapter 14

1. Joanna Glasner, "Startups Are Still Buying Fewer Startups," *Crunchbase News*, March 8, 2024, https://news.crunchbase.com/ma/large-cap-tech-startup-acquisitions-decline.
2. WFE Statistics Team, "IPO Trends," World Foundation of Exchanges, May 2024, https://focus.world-exchanges.org/articles/ipo-trends.

Acknowledgments

This book is a product of hundreds of amazing individuals who together form our greatest asset. We are humbled to have the opportunity to acknowledge some of them here.

Sincere gratitude to the incredible employees of LeadMD, our tribe. Through grit, determination, and the most unique skill sets found in Business-to-Business (B2B), for over 10 years we fought against the traditional misgivings about scale, and won. Never compromising quality, a small consultancy out of Arizona became the most successful GTM consultancy in its chosen markets. Beyond that, it changed the lives of everyone involved, perhaps none so much as ours for having known you.

To the partners and friends that made LeadMD great, your friendship and grace gave us the pedestal we stood on to reach our goals. Without your help, we would have been just another boutique consultancy – the rising tide lifts all ships.

We would also like to thank our incredible investors and portfolio companies at In Revenue Capital. Your trust and belief have enabled us to apply the Go-to-Market skills we love, while participating in a space where no two days look the same, and applying a partner-first mentality that requires your absolute confidence. The ride has been incredible so far, and is just getting started.

Also, to the incredible ecosystem being created around, well, partnership ecosystems – you are truly the most uncommon and supportive community to ever grace B2B. By sharing a like mindset, we share everything. The fundamentals of "give-to-get" are exemplified every day within this growing and thriving community, simply because we all believe in surrounding ourselves with great people and then doing everything possible to lift each other up. Thank you.

In that vein, to the dozens of partnership executives and leaders who contributed to this book in the form of interviews, quotes, podcast appearances, and conversations – we could not have done this without your help and insight.

Finally, to our wives – Jen and Meghan – without whom we would have been plagued with working 9 to 5s long ago. You are living saints who allow us the freedom to enter unfamiliar spaces armed only with your belief and the sheer will to succeed. The belief alone is always enough.

About the Authors

Justin Gray

Justin Gray is a five-time award-winning entrepreneur who has made a career of founding and scaling companies to successful personal exits of over $250 million. One of those ventures was LeadMD, a Go-to-Market and revenue operations consultancy that helped over 4000 Business-to-Business companies, ranging from high-growth start-ups to Fortune 500 enterprises, succeed through innovative strategy, technology, and tactics.

Now, as co-founder and managing director of In Revenue Capital, Justin couples Go-to-Market expertise with venture funding to empower seed stage founders and their startups through a first-of-its-kind model called Operator-Immersive capital.

Justin and his wife, Jennifer, met over marketing, have a son named like a superhero, Grayson, and a daughter, Declan, who's destined to be a rock star. When not driving revenues, you can find him driving a tractor at his hemp farm in Missouri or golf cart through the Arizona desert looking for a poorly executed tee shot.

Josh Wagner

Josh Wagner is a sales, marketing, and channel leader who has spent 20 years selling to and through strategic partners and has helped multiple startups scale from $0–$20 million. Today Josh is the cofounder and partner at In Revenue Capital, where he provides GTM operator expertise to support growth stage founders. Josh believes that ecosystem-led growth is the "cheat code" to revenue, enabling leaders to tap into one-to-many partner relationships to create more scale with fewer resources.

Josh and his wife, Meghan, have three children who keep them busy with school, sports, and extracurricular activities. When not in revenue, Josh can be found in his sanctuary (his home gym), on the golf course, or on the slopes.

Index

Page numbers followed by *f* refer to figures.

account-based marketing (ABM), 191

account executives (AEs)
  compensation for, 96
  in co-sell cycles, 132
  at customer events, 107
  from Marketo, 153–5, 157–8, 162
  planning with, 99
  responsibilities of, 93
  at road shows, 109
  from Salesforce, 133–5

account mapping, 20, 192

acquisition(s)
  definition of, 192
  effect on relationships, 139
  of LeadMD, 181
  and partnerships, 177–80
  potential of, 179–80
  of SaaS, 178*f*
  sales' role in, 31, 73
  successful exits by, 15, 174–5, 179
  of TOPO, 182–3
  venture capital's role in, 168
  see also mergers and acquisitions (M&A)

ACV, 149 *see* average contract value

Adler, Allan, 19, 44, 82

Adobe, 150–2

AEs *see* account executives

Albro, Scott, 183

annual contract value, 37, 56

annual recurring revenue (ARR), 144, 162

application programming interfaces (APIs), 166

Arizona State University (ASU), 2

average contract value (ACV), 37, 56, 145, 149

Bessemer Venture Partners, 21
better together message, 52, 60,
    78, 109, 121, 126, 130–1
blockbuster movie model, 25
board meetings, 122, 157,
    158–60
Boiler Room (film), 22
bowtie sales funnel, 82, 83*f*
Brinker, Scott, 42
business-to-business (B2B)
    digital tactics of, 11, 13
    and events, 110–11
    growth of, 44, 187
    inferior content from, x, 22
    marketing by, 9
    in paradigm shifts, 7–9
    in partner ecosystems, 41–2
    partnerships in, 20, 127
    performance recognition
        programs in, 106
    trust in, xi
    use of account mapping by, 20
buy-ins
    in comprehensive business
        cases, 156
    executive, 5, 39, 51, 128–9,
        167, 169, 171, 188–9
    need for, 30, 154
    securing, 157–8
    and three Cs framework, 79
    top-down, 127

CAC (customer acquisition cost),
    x, 142–7, 192
CEOs
    customer relations with, 101
    and ecosystems, 29–30
    in partnerships, 31, 33–4,
        70–1, 167
    visibility and leadership of,
        34–9
cheat codes
    ecosystem growth as, 200
    and events, 110
    and executive buy-in, 128–9
    and field activation, 52
    and growth, 19–27
    for GTM growth, 127, 178
    hub-and-spoke management
        model of, 42–4
    ideal partner profile (IPP)
        framework in, 44–9
    JVP in, 90, 130
    and partnership models, 41–2
    partnerships as, 27, 180
    and referrals, 60
    set up of, 41–53, 134
    and trust, 93
churn, 34, 37, 39, 71–2, 89, 93–4,
    145, 192
CLV *see* customer lifetime value
collaborative culture, 188–9
co-marketing, 32, 48, 91–100, 101

comprehensive business cases, 156–7

context aspect of three Cs, 62–70
    jobs-to-be-done (JTBD)
        framework in, 63–5
    meaningful outcomes in, 65–70

Contra (video game), 19

co-selling
    attempting, 79
    building, 166
    of complementary products, 169
    fostering, 166
    marketing, 96, 167
    in practice, 170–1
    value engineering vs., 94
    value of, 162

COVID-19, 12, 182

CRM *see* customer relationship management (CRM) systems

CSMs (customer success managers), 74, 89

culture aspect of three Cs, 62–70
    and Marketo partnership, 71–5
    in portfolio companies, 75–8
    referrals in, 78–9

culture fit, 47–9

customer acquisition cost (CAC), x, 142–7, 192

customer aspect of three Cs, 58–62

customer-centric approach, 188

customer lifetime value (CLV), 143–7, 150, 192

customer relationship management (CRM) systems, 36, 44, 64, 68, 131–2, 134–5, 193

customer(s)
    -centric approach, 188
    culture fit for, 48–9
    ecosystem of, 51
    events for, 107–8
    in field activation, 101–3
    and fleet management, 79–80
    joint solutions for, 128–31
    and JVP, 52
    life-cycle models of, 82–3
    marketing to, 32, 72–4, 85–7
    needs of, 61–2, 64–5
    in partner ecosystems, 42–4, 63
    partner potential of, 92–5
    in portfolio companies, 75–8
    proximity to, 50, 82
    relationships with, 20–1, 122
    roadshows for, 108–10
    sales' relationship to, 31
    solution fit for, 46–7
    success with, 33, 38–9, 88–90
    trust from, 15–18, 66, 81

customer success managers (CSMs), 74, 89
customer success teams, 98, 169

Digital Bridge Partners, 44, 82
digital marketing, 6, 9, 11, 16, 24, 74, 152, 182
digital mask, 17–18
  and customer trust, 15–18
  definition of, 192
  digital tactics in, 11
  importance of trust in, 10–11
  and technological paradigm shift, 7–10
digital tactics, 11–15
  and consumer wisdom, 13–14
  of startups, 14–15
  traditional vs., 12–13
discovery process, 94, 133, 153, 154, 157–8
Dreamforce, 50–1

earnings before interest, taxes, depreciation, and amortization (EBITDA), 14, 182
e-learning, 2–3
emotional intelligence, 140
Engagio, ix
EULER, 23, 95
ExactTarget, 132

exits
  acquisition of startups as, 174
  via acquisitions, 15, 174–5, 179
  in acquisitions vs. IPOs, 177
  definition of, 192
  through strategic partnerships, 180

field activation, 52, 101–2, 130
field activities, 101–15
  appreciation trips and awards as, 105–6
  customer events as, 107–8
  in-person events as, 104, 108, 111
  large events as, 110–14
  onsite visits as, 103–4
  road shows as, 108–10
  team-based dinners as, 104–5
financial lift model, 159
firmographic fit, 46
fleet management, 76–7
Forrester, 20
Fuller, Jared, 21, 35, 41, 50
fund dynamics, 23, 173–5, 175f

Gholston, Cassandra, 50–1
give-to-get mindset, 22–5, 50–1, 124, 129, 132, 198
Goldstein, Lauren, 90

growth
business-to-business, 44, 187
changing narrative of, 22
and cheat codes, 19–27
efficient, 26–7
and giving to get mindset,
22–5
in partnership ecosystem,
19–21
within partnerships, 27
of revenue, 17
The GTM Cheat Code podcast,
20, 30, 35, 50, 56, 70

hub-and-spoke management
model, 42–4, 43*f*, 49
HubSpot, 20, 36, 42

iBM, xi
ideal customer profile (ICP),
44–6, 45*f*, 52–3, 58, 99,
102, 129–30, 179
ideal partner profile (IPP)
framework, 44–9, 45*f*
culture fit, 47–9
firmographic fit, 46
setting up, 129
solution fit, 46–7
Impartner, 50–1
inbound marketing strategy
attractiveness of, 61–2, 145
definition of, 192

diminishing effect of, 144
direct sales in, 26–7
failure of digital in, 22
fluctuations in, 141
ineffectiveness of, 70
in partner ecosystems, 49, 83,
85–6
problems with, 11
purpose of, 9
see also outbound marketing
strategy
influenced revenue, 37–8, 48,
146–7
initial public offerings (IPOs),
173–5, 177, 184
In Revenue Capital, 22, 44, 165,
173
IPP *see* ideal partner profile
(IPP) framework

jobs-to-be-done (JTBD) framework, 60, 63–5, 65*f*, 77
joint value proposition (JVP)
assembling, 75
in culture, 71
customer-based, 90, 130,
188
definition of, 52–3
importance of, 37
in near term plans, 99
value of, 67
see also value propositions

Kester, Sean, 165
key performance indicators
      (KPIs), 31, 37, 123–4

lead life cycle, 68, 192
LeadMD
  acquisition of, 181–5
  better together message
     of, 52
  CSM's use of, 89
  customer evaluation by, 64
  exit of, 26
  field activation by, 101
  JVP at, 75–6, 90
  KPI referrals to, 124
  launch of, 11
  marketing at, 32, 85–8, 96
  and Microsoft, 27
  partner integration at, 82
  partnership with Marketo,
     71–5, 120–2, 159
  problem solving at, 60
  recognition programs
     of, 106
  referral fees at, 69
  revenue for, 162
  sponsorship of, 105
  traditional tactics at, 12
  use of outcomes by, 81
Leese, Scott, 17
lifetime value (LTV) *see* customer
     lifetime value (CLV)

M&A *see* mergers and acquisi-
     tions (M&A)
McBain, Jay, 20
McKinsey & Company, 19, 63
marketing *see* inbound marketing
     strategy; outbound
     marketing strategy
Marketo
  acquisition by Adobe, 150–1
  credibility of, 154–5
  field activities of, 101–14
  marketing of, 26–7, 85–8
  objection handling of, 152–4
  partnership with, 71–5
  relation with Salesforce, 132–5
Marketo maturity model, 87
mergers and acquisitions (M&A),
     175, 177–80, 192 *see also*
     acquisition(s)
Microsoft, 21, 26, 27, 29, 152–7,
     162, 178

narratives, 18, 22, 56, 109, 174,
     176
Nearbound: The Book (Fuller),
     35
Nearbound podcast, 35, 61
Nintendo, 19

objection handling, 156–63
  at board meetings, 158–60
  buy-in and discovery in, 157–8

comprehensive business case
for, 156–7
deals in, 162–3
high stakes of, 161
sales process credibility in,
154–5
use of, 98
onboarding, 83, 88–9, 168
operationalizing relationships,
188
operator-immersive capital, 16
operator immersive
model, 25
outbound marketing strategy
definition of, 192
diminishing effect of, 144
direct sales in, 26–7
dislike of, 61–2
failure of digital in, 22
fluctuations in, 141
ineffectiveness of, 70
inefficiency of, 145
in partner ecosystems, 49, 83,
86–8
problems with, 11
purpose of, 9
see also inbound marketing
strategy

PandaDoc, 36
Pardot, 132–4
partner compensation, 37–9

partner ecosystems, 19–21, 35,
37, 165, 168, 193
at Adobe, 150–2
components of, 81–90
customer success in,
89–90
inbound marketing in,
85–6
methodology of, 84f
onboarding in, 88–9
outbound marketing in,
86–8
strategies for, 167–8
PartnerHacker, 21
The Partner Hacker Handbook
(Fuller), 35
partner programs, 165–72
co-selling in, 170–1
creating successful, 168–9
misalignment in, 131–5
partnership ecosystems
strategy in, 167–8
partnership/sales balance in,
166–7
at Salesloft, 165–6
top alignment in, 169–70
partners
curating, 59–62, 64
definition of, 20
Partnership Leaders, 30, 79
partnership model, 41–2,
176–85

partnerships
    and acquisitions, 177–80
    collaborative culture in,
        188–9
    compensation within, 37–9
    customer-centric approach in,
        188
    marketing, 95–100
    as Microsoft cheat code, 27
    misalignment in, 131–5
    objection handling in, 152–63
    scaling, 98–9, 114
    siloed, 33–4
    strategic (*see* strategic
        partnerships)
    as strategic growth levers, 188
    successful, 149–63
    success metrics for, 141–7
PartnerTap, 50
partner win wire, 97*f*
performance recognition
        programs, 106
pipeline for life mindset, 138–9,
        141
pipelines
    communicating about, 170
    creating, 103, 107
    definition of, 193
    and partnerships, 112
    prospecting for, 98
Pitstop, 76–7, 78
Pitstop triangle, 77*f*

portfolio companies, 58, 64,
        75–8, 110, 168
Portnoy, Greg, 23, 95
power law, 175, 175*f*
productization-centric thinking, 63
product mentality, 63–4
proximity
    to customers, 21, 50–1, 82
    to ideal customer profile
        (ICP), 129–30
    to sellers, 103
    value of, 118–20
proxy perceptions, 32
pull marketing *see* outbound
        marketing strategy
push marketing *see* inbound
        marketing strategy

quarterly business reviews
        (QBRs), 104–6

referrals, 78–9
    agreements for, 49, 149
    fees for, 69, 193
    as metric, 167
    one-way, 48
    as partner programs, 131
relational mindset, 120–2
relationships, 117–26
    failures of, 127–35
    operationalizing, 188
    partnerships in, 20

and proximity, 118–20
relational mindset in, 120–2
value adding in, 125–6
value proposition
    reinforcement in, 122–5
return on investment (ROI), 80,
    111–12, 125, 142, 144,
    158–9, 166–7, 170
Reveal, 35, 41
road shows, 108–10
Rosenberg, Craig, 183
Rowley, Jill, 51, 61

SaaS *see* software-as-a-service
    (SaaS)
sales development
    representatives (SDRs),
    ix–x, 22
sales engagement, x, 193
Salesforce.com, 25, 51
sales kickoffs (SKOs), 74, 105–6,
    123
Salesloft, 165–8
sales process, 13, 33, 68, 154–5,
    157, 193
sales qualified lead (SQL), 29,
    193
Samila, Chris, 30, 79
scaling, 98–9, 114
Scott Leese Consulting, 17
SDRs (sales development
    representatives), ix–x, 22

Shopify, 20
software-as-a-service (SaaS),
    21–2, 29, 82, 144,
    149–50, 162, 178*f*, 181–2
solution fit, 46–7
solution overlap, 59–61
sourced revenue, 37–8, 48,
    146–7
sponsorship, 105–6, 111–12, 123
SQL (sales qualified lead), 29,
    193
Stage 2 Capital, 51, 61
Stanford University, 25
startups
    acquisition of, 174
    ingredients of, 23
    landscape of, 14–15
    in partnership ecosystem, 29
    ROI of, 170
    in traditional venture model,
        176
    use of ICPs by, 58
strategic partnerships
    average number of, 16
    communication in, 119, 122
    definition of, 193
    exits through, 180
    growth through, 187
    investing in, xi, 73
    in partner ecosystems, 193
    value proposition
        reinforcement in, 122–3

Strategyn, 63
success metrics, 137–46
    customer acquisition cost
        (CAC) in, 142–3
    customer lifetime value (CLV)
        in, 143–7
    for partnerships, 141–7
    and trust, 137–41

technographic analysis, 87, 193
technological paradigm shift,
    7–10
telematics, 76–8
three Cs of marketing
    framework, 55–80, 57*f*
top-down organization, 29–39
    roles in, 30–4
    visibility and leadership in,
        34–9
TOPO, 182–3
traditional venture model,
    173–6, 177
trust
    and B2B growth, 187
    of customers, 15–18

emotional intelligence in, 140
as a foundation, 137–41
importance of, 10
outward focus in, 140
pipeline for life mindset in,
    138–9

UC Berkeley, 25
Ulwick, Tony, 63

value propositions, 61, 77, 119,
    122–5, 168 *see also* joint
    value proposition (JVP)
venture capital (VC)
    and giving to get mindset,
        22–3
    investments by, 14–15
    partnership model of,
        176–85
    perceived impact of, 24*f*
    traditional model of, 173–6
visibility, 34–5, 62, 106, 112, 131,
    147

Winning by Design, 90